Leaders of the Colonial Era

William Penn

Leaders of the Colonial Era

Lord Baltimore

Benjamin Banneker

William Bradford

Benjamin Franklin

Anne Hutchinson

Cotton Mather

William Penn

John Smith

Miles Standish

Peter Stuyvesant

Leaders of the Colonial Era

William Penn

Joanne Mattern

CHELSEA HOUSE
PUBLISHERS

An imprint of Infobase Publishing

Chelsea House
An imprint of Infobase Publishing
132 West 31st Street
New York, NY 10001

Library of Congress Cataloging-in-Publication Data
Mattern, Joanne, 1963–
  William Penn / Joanne Mattern.
    p. cm. — (Leaders of the Colonial era)
  Includes bibliographical references and index.
  ISBN 978-1-60413-735-4 (hardcover)
  1. Penn, William, 1644–1718—Juvenile literature. 2. Pioneers—Pennsylvania—
Biography—Juvenile literature. 3. Quakers—Pennsylvania—Biography—Juvenile
literature. 4. Pennsylvania—History—Colonial period, ca. 1600–1775—Juvenile
literature. I. Title. II. Series.
  F152.2.M38 2010
  974.8'02092—dc22
  [B]   2010026366

You can find Chelsea House on the World Wide Web at
http://www.chelseahouse.com.

Text design by Kerry Casey
Cover design by Keith Trego
Composition by EJB Publishing Services
Cover printed by Bang Printing, Brainerd, Minn.
Book printed and bound by Bang Printing, Brainerd, Minn.
Date printed: December 2010
Printed in the United States of America

10 9 8 7 6 5 4 3 2 1

This book is printed on acid-free paper.

Contents

1

The Admiral's Son

In England during the middle of the seventeenth century, few men were as important as William Penn Sr. Penn was a sea captain and a favorite of the British king. He had high hopes that his oldest son, who was also named William, would follow in his footsteps. However, for many years, father and son did not get along. The younger William was outspoken and followed a controversial religion. His father must have despaired that his son would carry on the family's good name.

However, William Sr. need not have worried about his son's future. William Penn would go on to become one of the most important and forward-thinking men of his time. His beliefs and actions would affect the course of a new nation and bring him fame that lasted long past his death.

THE PENN FAMILY

William Penn was born on October 14, 1644. His father was only twenty-three years old, but he was already well known in royal circles. He had been a sailor since he was a young boy and had quickly risen through the ranks to become an officer when he was in his late teens. The younger Penn later wrote that his father was "addicted from his youth to maritime affairs."

When his son was born, William Penn Sr. was captain of a British man-of-war vessel called the *Fellowship*. The ship was scheduled to sail to Ireland, but its departure was delayed for two weeks so William Sr. could be with his wife, Margaret, and their newborn son. On October 23, baby William was baptized at All Hallows Church on Tower Street in London, just around the corner from the Penns' house. A few days later, Captain Penn and the *Fellowship* left for Ireland.

Margaret Penn was often lonely during the years after William's birth. Her husband was away for much of the child's first five years, fighting against rebels in Ireland. Margaret and William lived in a small house on Tower Hill, near the Tower of London, a famous prison. The house had "one hall and parlor and kitchen with a divided cellar . . . and above stairs in the first story two fair chambers and in the second story two more chambers and two garrets over the same with a yard before."

Although Margaret may have struggled during those early years without her husband, she had faced hardship before. Margaret was the daughter of a London businessman. When she was a teenager, she married a Dutch merchant named Nicasius van der Schuren, and they lived with her family in Ireland until her husband died of illness just a year later. Soon afterward, in 1641, war broke out between Irish Catholics and Protestants, and Margaret and her father fled to London, where Margaret met and married Captain Penn. Their son was born a little more than a year later.

Margaret was a fun-loving woman who enjoyed spending time with family and friends more than she cared for keeping house. Samuel Pepys, a famous writer who kept a diary about daily life in England during this time and who was a close friend and neighbor of the Penns, once wrote about Margaret's casual style. Pepys stated that Margaret walked around her house "with her stockings hanging round her heels." He also complained about the "plain cooking" that was served at the Penns' house whenever he and his wife were invited to dinner. Another contemporary writer described Margaret as "happy-go-lucky, fond of a frolick, and remarkably untidy."

Margaret may have been untidy, but she was a loving mother. Young William was generally a healthy child, although he did suffer from smallpox when he was three years old. This disease was very common during the 1600s, especially in places like London that had crowded, dirty conditions. Although many people died from smallpox or were permanently disfigured, William survived. However, he did lose most of his hair as a result of his illness and wore a wig for the rest of his life.

William Penn Sr. was an admiral for the British Royal Navy and was knighted by King Charles II. His close ties with King Charles II would greatly impact his son William as well as the future state of Pennsylvania.

CIVIL WAR

The mid-1600s were a turbulent and violent time in Great Britain. The nation was ruled by King

THE DANGERS OF LIFE IN LONDON

London in the 1600s was not a pleasant place to live. People lived in houses that were jammed together along narrow streets. It was very easy for disease to spread in this environment. Two of the deadliest diseases at the time were smallpox, which caused high fevers, headaches, and a skin rash that often left disfiguring scars, and the bubonic plague, which was also called the Black Death. The close confines of the city also made fire an ever-present danger. In 1666, the Great Fire of London burned for three days and destroyed thirteen thousand homes.

The city was dirty and smelly. People dumped their garbage—including human waste, because there was no indoor plumbing—into the street or into the Thames River. Rats and other vermin lived in buildings or on the streets. Coal or wood fires were used to heat homes and cook food, so the air was filled with smoke, making it hard to breathe. It's no wonder the Penns wanted to move to the country!

Charles I. Charles I often fought with the members of Parliament and tried to get them to enact laws they didn't support. In 1642 the nation plunged into civil war, with most of the nobility and the peasant classes supporting the king, while the middle class, including tradesmen and merchants, supported Parliament. In 1649 the members of Parliament had Charles I arrested and executed. Charles's sons fled to France and lived in exile for the next 21 years.

Oliver Cromwell, an outspoken member of Parliament who had led several successful military campaigns against Charles I, became the ruler of England after Charles's execution. Cromwell declined to be named king but ruled England under the title of Lord Protector of the Commonwealth. Although the nation was technically ruled by a Council of State made up of army officers and civilians, Cromwell was a dictator and his word was law.

Life during Cromwell's reign was not much fun. Cromwell and the members of Parliament practiced a religion called Puritanism. Puritans were very strict and did not allow public celebrations or other expressions of joy. Sports were banned, as were other "frivolous" amusements such as circuses, music, and theater. Sundays were spent in church, and it was illegal to travel or work on that day. England became a dreary, joyless place under Cromwell's rule.

Captain William Penn faced a difficult decision when Oliver Cromwell came to power. He was a Royalist, or someone who supported the king, and he had been close friends with King Charles's family for years. However, Penn knew that he had to follow Cromwell's orders if he wanted to keep his position in the Royal Navy. Fortunately for Captain Penn, he was very good at politics and managed to win a lot of favor with Cromwell. Over the next few years, Penn spent most of his time at sea, fighting the rebels in Ireland. He was so successful at putting down uprisings along the coast of Ireland that Cromwell promoted Penn and gave him the title of Rear Admiral of the Irish Seas. His new position paid more money and allowed Penn to move his family from dirty, dangerous, overcrowded London into a house in the country.

An Eventful Childhood

When he was young, William Penn did not see much of his father. He and his mother lived in London while his father sailed the Irish seas. The family was not happy in London, which was filthy, crowded, dangerous, and disease ridden. Admiral Penn saved his pay, along with his share of the treasures he found at sea. The whole family was delighted when they could finally afford to leave the city. When William was about five years old, the family moved to Wanstead, a country town just outside of London. Soon after the move, the Penns welcomed a daughter, William's sister, Margaret.

LIFE IN THE COUNTRY

When William was about six years old, he enrolled in school. William attended a small school in the nearby village of Chigwell, four miles away from his home. The Free Grammar School was founded in 1629 by Dr. Samuel Harsnett, who was also the vicar, or minister, of Chigwell. Harsnett was determined that his students would not only be well educated but would also have a strong spiritual foundation. He told his teachers to be sure that "the buds of virtue were stirred up" in their students. Harsnett said, "I charge my schoolmasters . . . that they bring up their scholars in the fear of God and reverence toward all men: and that they teach them obedience to their parents, observance to their betters . . . and above all that they chastise them severely for three vices—lying, swearing, and filthy speaking." Students who broke the rules were beaten with a thin wooden cane, a common practice in schools of that time. Teachers also had to follow a strict code of conduct. They were told to show "only grave behavior" to their students and to be "severe in discipline."

Schooldays at Chigwell were very long. During the summer, William arrived at school at six o'clock in the morning and stayed until six o'clock at night every day except for Sunday. Winter hours were slightly shorter. During the winter, William attended school from seven in the morning until five in the afternoon, with a two-hour break in the middle of the day. He did this almost every day until he was twelve years old.

Admiral Penn wanted to make sure his son had a fine education that would prepare him for life as a gentleman and a businessman. William learned to read and write, and he also studied grammar, spelling, and math. Later, his lessons included Latin, Greek, advanced mathematics, science, history, and religion. Students learned by repeating lessons over and over or by copying them out of books. There was little room for creativity or personal expression.

William did well at school and enjoyed his time there. By the age of eleven he could read and write in Latin and Greek and speak some French. He had an excellent memory and spent a lot of time studying.

School also gave William the chance to interact with other boys his age, which was something new for a child who had spent most of his childhood at home with his mother. Although most of the students at the Chigwell school were from upper-class families, Harsnett also gave scholarships to about a dozen needy students every year. For the first time, William became friends with the sons of farmers, laborers, and tradesmen. It was probably at this time that he began to feel compassion for those who were not as fortunate as he was.

Although school took up a great deal of William's time, there were also many opportunities to have fun. The countryside was full of interesting places to explore, and William no doubt spent hours playing in the fields and woods of his home, developing a love of nature that lasted all of his life. He was a fine athlete and was especially good at foot races. Stories say that as soon as he heard the school bell in the morning, William would run the four miles from his home to school and always arrived on time. Chores at home also kept William busy, since almost all household jobs were done by hand. When his father returned from his journeys William would listen excitedly to his tales of adventures on the high seas.

In 1652 young William had one of the most exciting times of his childhood. War had broken out between Great Britain and the newly formed Republic of the Netherlands because the Netherlands was challenging England's power at sea. Admiral Penn and his fleet went into battle and scored a huge victory at the Battle of Texel. Great Britain was overwhelmed by a rush of pride and excitement, which was especially welcome in the joyless days of Puritanism. Penn became a national hero and was promoted to General-of-the-Sea, which was the highest rank possible for a naval officer. Oliver Cromwell personally presented Penn with a gold chain to hang around his

As reward for his remarkable achievements at sea against the Netherlands, William Penn's father was given the Macroom estate, including Macroom Castle (*above*), in England.

neck, as well as a large estate called Macroom, which was located in County Cork, Ireland. Cromwell said the estate was given to Penn as a reward for his "good and faithful services performed to the Commonwealth." It seemed that Admiral Penn was a favorite of Cromwell's. However, fortunes could change quickly in Great Britain, and that's exactly what happened to Penn.

SHOCKING CHARGES

In 1655, when he was eleven years old, William's life changed dramatically. His father was in deep trouble. The family received the shocking news that Admiral Penn's superiors had accused him of disobeying orders, arrested him, and locked him up in the Tower of London. The family rushed to London to find out what was going on.

Oliver Cromwell, the Lord Protector and ruler of England, had sent Admiral Penn, along with a band of soldiers and an army general, to the island of Hispaniola in the Caribbean Sea. Their goal was to take the island and claim it for Great Britain. However, the island's natives had fought back more violently than the English had expected, and the soldiers were unable to take control of the island. Admiral Penn decided to take control of the island of Jamaica instead. Jamaica had more resources than Hispaniola and was also full of pirates. By capturing the island, Penn and his men were able to gain riches for England and get rid of the pirates, making the Caribbean safe for shipping.

Although it seemed like Admiral Penn had done good work, Cromwell was angry that he had not followed orders and had seized Jamaica without official permission. As far as Cromwell was concerned, Penn had committed treason. Instead of the honors and rewards Penn had expected for finding good in a bad situation, Cromwell charged him with disobeying orders and threw him into prison.

Taking power after the death of King Charles, Oliver Cromwell (*above*) led England as a republic, making him the country's first civilian leader. Although Cromwell had rewarded Sir William Penn, he soon threw him into the Tower of London for treason.

Admiral Penn spent five long weeks imprisoned in the Tower of London. Margaret and the children moved back into their old house at Tower Hill to be close to him. Penn was questioned many times by Cromwell's men. Cromwell wanted to prove that Penn had deliberately disobeyed orders, but all his questioning came to nothing. Cromwell was unable to prove his accusations, and he knew that he could not leave a person as important and beloved in jail without a trial. Finally, Cromwell let Admiral Penn go free, but he stripped the admiral of his naval command.

Admiral Penn decided that he'd had enough of working for Cromwell. He was a smart man who understood politics and could tell when change was in the air. He realized that Cromwell's days as Lord Protector would soon be over. He decided the smartest thing to do was leave London and settle at the Irish estate Cromwell had given him just a few years earlier.

OFF TO IRELAND

On August 12, 1656, the Penn family moved to Macroom Castle in Ireland. Macroom had been the site of a major battle between Oliver Cromwell's army and forces commanded by King Charles I. The castle was a huge fortress meant to protect the large estate and the villagers that lived in simple thatched houses nearby. For several years, Admiral Penn had rented out the land to farmers and used their rents as a source of income. Now Macroom would not only be an investment, it would be the family's home.

Family life was good at Macroom Castle. A second son, Richard, was born to the family. Even better, in young William's opinion, was that his father was no longer away from home for months on end. Instead, Admiral Penn was home more often and spent a lot of time with William Jr. Since William was the oldest son, the admiral expected him to take over as head of the family one day. To help him become successful, the admiral taught William valuable skills, such as how to manage an estate, how to fight, and how to act like a

THE QUAKERS

The Quakers are a religious group founded in Great Britain during the 1650s. The group is also called the Religious Society of Friends. Quakers were dissatisfied with existing religious denominations and promoted a more direct experience with God that was available without going to the clergy or receiving sacraments. George Fox, one of the co-founders of the Quakers, wrote in his *Journal*, that "Christ has come to teach His people Himself." Quakers act on this belief by worshiping God in their own way. During their religious services, called meetings, people usually sit quietly until one of them feels compelled to speak.

Quakers seek a simple life and turn away from fancy clothes and unnecessary possessions. They also do not believe in wars and usually refuse to fight. In Penn's time, Quakers refused to remove their hats in the presence of the nobility, which was a common sign of showing respect, because they believed everyone was equal. Many people thought the Quakers were a threat to the established society and the church and feared their radical ideas about God's relationship to humans, as well as their refusal to obey government rules that they felt conflicted with their religious beliefs. These fears and misunderstandings led to intense persecution of Quakers for many years.

gentleman. The two spent many hours together, and William learned a lot from his father.

A NEW KIND OF RELIGION

At twelve years old, William was a serious boy. One friend described him as "mighty lively, but . . . delighted in retirement [solitude]."

William spent a lot of time alone, often reading the Bible and other religious books for hours each day. He thought about God and meditated.

One day, William had his first religious revelation. He was alone in his bedroom when he was "suddenly surprised with an inward comfort and . . . an external glory that convinced him not only that God existed but also that he could communicate with Him, could know His will, and feel His peace." William was also convinced that God was calling him to take up a holy life. William later called this experience an "awakening" and the beginning of his spiritual life.

At thirteen years old, William was searching for spiritual under-standing. At that time, William had his first experience with the Quaker religion. This experience shaped the rest of his life. Quak-ers were a new and controversial religious group in Great Britain. Admiral Penn wanted to learn more about the Quakers, so he invited a traveling preacher named Thomas Loe to speak at Macroom Castle. Penn's family, villagers, and members of the castle's staff all gathered in a large room to hear Loe speak. "Let us hear before we judge," Admiral Penn advised.

William was mesmerized by Loe's descriptions of the Quakers and their beliefs. Loe said that an "inner light" or spiritual sense was available to anyone, and that every man and woman could have a close relationship with God. William was deeply moved by Loe's speech. The preacher's words seemed to describe exactly what had happened to William during his spiritual awakening. William believed that God sometimes visited him in dreams. When he thought about the day he had felt a tremendous sense of peace and light in the room, he wondered if this was the "inner light" that Thomas Loe spoke of. From that day on, William thought about "the knowledge of God from the living witness."

Loe soon moved on to another town, but William continued to think about what the preacher had said. At that time, most religious practices were bound up in rituals and rules set down by authorities. William wanted a more personal relationship with God, and he thought the Quakers might offer that to him. When William grew up, he declared his simple faith by writing, "Religion is nothing else but love to God and man" and "To be like Christ is to be a Christian." The seeds of those writings were sown that day at Macroom Castle.

3

William's Rebellion

By 1660 the winds of change had swept across British politics again. In 1659 Oliver Cromwell died and was succeeded by his son. Richard Cromwell did not have the strong personality of his father, and he was unable to govern a nation that was increasingly tired of all the Puritan restrictions and rules. In 1660 Richard resigned and Parliament invited Charles II to return as England's king. This event was called the Restoration, and it changed England—and the lives of the Penns—in a big way.

A ROYAL RETURN

In 1660, officials in Parliament invited Admiral Penn to return to England. They knew he had always supported the royal family and wanted him to be an important

After Oliver Cromwell's death, Charles II took over as king of England. Charles's coronation procession (*above*) was viewed by all of London, including the Penns.

part of the Restoration. The Penns were delighted to return to favor and left Macroom to move back to London. Soon afterward, in April 1660, Admiral Penn boarded a ship called the *Naseby* and sailed to Scheveningen, Holland, where Charles I's sons Charles, James, and Henry were living in exile. When Charles, now Charles II, king of England, boarded the ship to return home, one of the first things he did was make Admiral Penn a knight. From then on, he would be known as Sir William Penn.

The *Naseby*, renamed the *Royal Charles* after the new king, sailed back to England with the monarch and his brothers on board. Sir William Penn's son, William, joined the crowds in Dover, a port not far from London, to welcome his father and the new king home. One witness described the joyous scene at the dock as "a triumph of about 20,000 horses and foots, brandishing their swords and shouting with inexpressible joy; the waves strew'd with flowers, the bells ringing, the streets hung with tapistry, fountaines running with wine."

The Penns were present at Charles II's coronation in London in the spring of 1661. William and his parents went to a friend's house that was along the procession route from the Tower of London to Westminster Abbey, where the coronation would take place. Their friend Samuel Pepys was there, too. He described the scene: "So glorious was the show with gold and silver that we were unable to look at it, our eyes at last being so much overcome." It was truly a joyous day for London and for the Penn family.

OFF TO OXFORD

William Penn was sixteen when Charles II returned to England. Now that his father was restored to a position of favor, it was time for young Penn to complete his education and move into the position he would inherit as the son of one of England's most powerful noblemen. In October 1660, Penn enrolled at Christ Church College at Oxford University. Oxford was one of the oldest and best universities in England, and many young men from noble and important families attended the school. At the time Penn enrolled, there were about 2,500 students at Oxford, with about 100 of them studying at Christ Church College.

Penn was very eager to go to Oxford. He had not attended school for several years, instead studying at home with private tutors. Although this was common for the sons of the nobility, it wasn't enough for Penn. He was very smart and wanted more of a challenge when it came to his education. Going to Oxford would provide more intellectual opportunities, and this was just what Penn wanted. During his first year, Penn studied history and philosophy. He read works by great classical writers such as Plutarch, Plato, and Aristotle, as well as more modern works by philosophers such as Erasmus and Descartes.

Penn enjoyed the intellectual challenges of Oxford, but in other ways, life at the school was very upsetting to him. After the Restoration and the return of King Charles II, people turned away from the strict Puritan rules and way of life. Many of the young men who were students at Oxford got carried away as they enjoyed their new freedoms. They spent much of their time partying and drinking, or roaming the streets at night and getting into fights. Penn was disgusted at this behavior. He later wrote that Oxford and other universities were "signal places for idleness, looseness, prophaneness, prodigality, and gross ignorance." He also called his time at Oxford "hellish darkness and debauchery."

Many of the students at Oxford also acted as if they were better than other people. They were intolerant and often bullied groups or people who did not conform to society's rules. One of their main targets was the Quakers. Penn often witnessed his classmates harassing and even beating Quakers they found preaching in public.

The authorities did nothing to stop this because the new government and many citizens shared the students' contempt and anger at the Quakers and other religious groups. The government even passed rules stating that everyone had to worship in the Church of England, also called the Anglican Church. Those who refused could be arrested, stoned, or beaten. For Penn, who believed in religious freedom and had been deeply moved when he heard Thomas Loe speak about his Quaker beliefs years before at Macroom, watching his classmates act so disrespectfully must have been very difficult. Instead of socializing, Penn withdrew more deeply into his studies. This upset his father, who felt that Penn had always been too sheltered. Sir William wanted his son to experience more of the world and become what he considered to be a responsible member of society.

PENN IN TROUBLE

Penn left Oxford briefly during the spring of 1661 to take part in the activities surrounding the coronation of King Charles II. When he returned to school in October 1661, he was disappointed at what he found. The religious rules at Oxford had become even stricter than they'd been the year before. Students had to attend religious services and wear an outer garment called a surplice. Penn was not the only student who didn't like these rules, and he soon joined with other nonconformists. Penn also found inspiration from a former dean of Christ Church named Dr. John Owen. Owen had taught at Oxford until the Restoration, when he was forced to leave because the new administration did not like his independent ideas.

Owen could no longer teach at Oxford, but that didn't stop him from educating others. He set up classes at his home, and Penn was soon one of his most ardent followers. Owen believed in asking questions and being an independent thinker. Penn and Owen agreed that students should not have to follow the Anglican faith if they did not want to. Along with Owen's other followers, Penn refused to attend the required religious services at Oxford.

It didn't take long for the school authorities to notice that a group of students had stopped going to church. They ordered Penn and his friends to attend services and to stop going to Owen's house. Penn was outraged and felt that the university was forcing him to go against his own religious beliefs. He refused to give in and continued to visit Owen. Because of his disobedience, Penn was fined and formally reprimanded. He also faced an even harsher punishment when Oxford sent a letter to his father explaining what his son was doing.

Sir William could not believe that his son had gotten into trouble. He told Penn that he was risking his entire future by behaving so foolishly. He warned Penn that he would never gain favor with the king or be appointed to an important government position if he

John Owen's (*above*) ideas about religious freedom influenced the developing mind of William Penn. Penn's resistance to attending church services got him into trouble at Oxford and with his father.

didn't follow the rules of Oxford and if he continued to fight against the country's religious rules. Sir William decided Penn needed to take his mind off studying and religion. He sent for his son, and Penn spent several weeks in London, attending the theater and going to parties. After this break, Sir William sent his son back to Oxford, hoping that things would be different.

Penn loved his father, but he could not go against his own conscience. He continued to break Oxford's rules, and in March 1662 he was finally expelled for nonconformity. Penn made his way back to London to face his father. Sir William was furious. Penn later said he received "bitter usage" at his father's hands, including "whipping, beating, and turning out of doors." Sir William Penn kicked his son out of the house, and Penn was forced to stay with friends for a few nights. Finally, his mother, who had always been soft-hearted and protective of her oldest child, convinced Sir William to let Penn come back home.

Penn returned to the house on Tower Hill, but relations between him and his father were very tense. Samuel Pepys came to visit one day and later noted in his diary, "Walking in the garden with Sir W. Penn: his son William is at home, not well. But all things, I fear, do not go well with them—they look discontentedly, but I know not what ails them."

A TRIP TO FRANCE

Sir William Penn was seriously worried about his son's future. He decided the best thing to do was send Penn away from England entirely. At that time, most sons of noble families traveled to continental Europe, where they completed their education, learned about foreign affairs and politics, socialized with other gentlemen, and perhaps found a wife. In July 1662 Penn headed off to France, where he would spend the next two years.

KING LOUIS XIV

King Louis XIV was born in 1638 and became king of France when he was only four years old, upon the death of his father, King Louis XIII. Because he was so young, France was ruled by a regency council made up of Louis's mother and several noblemen, including Cardinal Jules Mazarin. Mazarin kept most of the power for himself and forced Louis to grow up in poverty. When Cardinal Mazarin died in 1661, 23-year-old Louis announced that he would rule by himself. For the next 54 years, he ruled France as an absolute monarch, with all power in the kingdom resting with him. King Louis XIV was a great lover of the arts and encouraged art, drama, music, and science. French culture became very advanced during his reign. He was called the Sun King and built the luxurious Palace of Versailles. King Louis XIV died in 1715. His 72-year reign was the longest in European history.

Penn quickly became part of the court of the French king, Louis XIV. The court of King Louis XIV was quite elaborate. Penn enjoyed life at court, which was full of amusements such as music, theater, and art. He also became very fond of French fashion and was soon dressing in fancy clothes and the latest styles. Fine clothes would be a favorite of Penn's for the rest of his life, despite the Quaker belief in plain and simple dress.

One night, however, Penn received a rude shock. As he walked home from a night at the theater, he passed a French nobleman. The nobleman lifted his hat as a sign of respect to Penn, but Penn didn't see him and didn't lift his hat in return. The nobleman, who was probably drunk, became angry at what he thought was an insult and drew his sword, ready to fight with Penn. Penn later wrote, "I will suppose he [might have] killed me for he made several passes at me [with his sword], or I in my defence [might have] killed him." Instead, Penn, who had been taught sword fighting by his father, quickly disarmed the man and apologized. The Frenchman left, but Penn was deeply troubled by the event. He realized that he could have killed a man, or been killed himself, just because he hadn't lifted his hat. "I ask any man of understanding or conscience if the whole ceremony were worth a man's life?" he wrote. To Penn, violence was not the answer.

Penn decided to go back to his religious studies. France was open to religious freedom, and Penn soon enrolled at a Protestant academy in the town of Saumur, a few miles from Paris. The school was run by Moses Amyraut, who was one of the most famous free thinkers of his time. Penn may well have heard about Amyraut from Dr. John Owen at Oxford. Amyraut taught his students that religious tolerance was important and that every individual had the right to personal freedom and to believe whatever he wanted. He also preached nonviolence and stated that a man's actions, particularly actions that helped others, were the only things that mattered. And he stated that everyone had an "inner light" that came from God and that this light should guide everything a person did.

Penn became close to Amyraut, even living in the teacher's house while he attended the school. Under Amyraut's guidance, and by following his own heart, Penn began developing the religious beliefs that would guide him for the rest of his life. He knew he would not follow the Anglican religion, but Penn did not yet have a clear idea if there was any organized religion that would meet his needs. All he knew was that his life and his way of thinking had changed a great deal from the young man who had left Oxford in disgrace just two years earlier.

4

Quaker Beliefs

Moses Amyraut died in 1664. Penn saw no reason to stay in France without his former teacher and friend, so he left the country and spent the next few months traveling around Europe. He felt he had matured in the two years he'd been away and that it was time to go home. That spring, 20-year-old Penn sailed for England and went back to his parents' house on Tower Hill.

PENN AT SEA

Penn's parents were happy to see him after two years apart and welcomed him home. Sir William was eager for his son to continue his education, so he enrolled him at a prestigious London law school called Lincoln's Inn. Penn began his studies there in February 1665 and did well. It was common for young noblemen to receive legal training during this time, as preparation for a future in business or government service. In addition, law school was seen as an excellent way to polish a gentleman's education and it provided social contacts that could be important in the future.

Penn enjoyed law school, but he was not able to spend very much time there. War had broken out between England and the Netherlands in 1664, shortly before Penn returned home. This war was triggered by England's capture of the Dutch colony of New Netherland (now New York) in North America. In April 1665 Sir William was called into action when his ship, the *Royal Charles*, commanded a fleet of 38 ships that was ordered to sail into combat against the Netherlands. Sir William took his son out of school and asked him to accompany him on the journey.

Going to sea with his father was an eye-opening experience for Penn. For the first time, he saw how much respect his father commanded from his crew and how loyal his men were to their leader. When the fleet sailed into combat, Penn was also able to see what a brilliant military leader his father was. Although Penn was only at sea for three weeks, the experience made him understand his father much more than he ever had before.

At the end of April, Sir William sent his son back to England with confidential messages for the king. This arrangement allowed the admiral to send someone he trusted with the news of battle and was also an excellent way to introduce his son to King Charles II. Sir William hoped his son would make a good impression, which might help him in the future.

The admiral's plan worked perfectly. When Penn arrived at the king's residence in London, Charles II was still in bed. When the king heard that a messenger had come from Sir William, he rushed to meet Penn, who later described how the king was "earnestly skipping out of his bed, he came only in his gown and slippers." Penn delivered his messages and left with the assurance that he had made a good and memorable impression on the king.

After Penn returned to England, he wrote a letter to his father that made it clear how much he had come to love and respect the older man. Things had clearly changed from the days when the two had quarreled over religion and responsibility. Penn wrote: "I pray God, after all the foul weather and dangers you are exposed to, and shall be, that you come home as secure. And I bless God, my heart does in any way fail, but firmly believe that if God has called you out to battle, He will cover your head in that smoky day. And I never knew what a father was till I had wisdom enough to prize him, so I can safely say, that now, of all times, your concerns are most dear to me."

THE PLAGUE

Penn did not return to the *Royal Charles* after his meeting with the king, but instead went back to his studies at Lincoln's Inn. But his stay at the school did not last long. In 1665 London was struck with an outbreak of a deadly disease called the bubonic plague. In order to slow the spread of the plague, most public places, including schools, were closed. Even so, the plague killed an estimated 70,000 people in London before the outbreak ended.

People were desperately afraid of the plague, which spread and killed its victims with devastating speed. People abandoned their own family members, and if neighbors knew someone who was sick, they would not go near the person's house to help him or her. Anyone who could afford to leave London did just that.

There was one exception to the abandonment of the sick and the dying. Penn was astonished when he found out that the Quakers did not shy away from helping the plague's victims. Instead of d Casualties this Week.

Imposthume	11
Infants	16
Killed by a fall from the Belfrey at Alhallows the Great	1
Kingsevil	2
Lethargy	1
Palsie	1
Plague	7165
Rickets	17
Rising of the Lights	11

This is a weekly death census from 1665, showing the plague to be the outstanding cause of deaths. The plague was responsible for more than 70,000 deaths in London.

fleeing the city, they actually went from door to door and entered the victims' houses to help them. Although there was no cure for the disease, the Quakers helped by bringing food and water to afflicted families and helping dispose of the dead with dignity, even though their actions led to many Quakers contracting the deadly disease. These acts occurred at a time when Quakers were still hated and persecuted. Meanwhile, ministers of the Church of England did nothing to help their parishioners. Penn was astonished at the Quakers' display of selflessness and shocked that ministers of other religions did little to help. He began to rethink his own life and ideals, and to move farther away from the life that was expected of him and closer to life as a Quaker. Later, Penn wrote, "In the time of the Great Plague in London, [the Lord] gave me deep sense . . . of the vanity of this world, of the irreligiousness of the religious in it."

The plague epidemic had run its course by October, and Penn returned again to Lincoln's Inn. Soon afterward, his father returned from the war with the Netherlands. Sir William and the king's brother, the Duke of York, defeated the Dutch in the English Channel. By then, Sir William's health was failing. He would never return to sea again, but instead accepted a desk job in the naval office in London.

OFF TO IRELAND

Now that he was retired from the sea, the admiral decided it was time for his son to take on more responsibilities. In 1665 Penn left Lincoln's Inn and went to work for his father. The first job Penn took on was as commissioner of a charity that supervised donations and assistance to the needy. Penn enjoyed this position very much. He gained experience in local politics and also had a chance to work firsthand with England's poor and take action to reduce their suffering. Penn held this position for less than a year. His father had decided that Penn should take on even bigger responsibilities.

Although the family had not lived there for years, the Penns still owned a large estate in Ireland. However, Macroom Castle and its lands had originally belonged to people who had been loyal to King Charles I. After Charles I was executed, his successor, Oliver Cromwell, gave the lands to the Penn family. Now that Charles I's son, Charles II, was king, his friends demanded their lands back, and Charles returned the estate to them. However, the king still valued Sir William, so he gave the family another estate, called Shangarry,

BUBONIC PLAGUE

Bubonic plague was also called "the Black Death" because its victims suffered from black spots on their bodies. The disease first appeared in China in the early 1330s and was spread to Europe within the next 20 years by traders and merchants. The plague was spread by fleas that bit infected rats that then bit people and infected them. The disease spread so rapidly and killed people so quickly that the Italian writer Giovanni Boccaccio said its victims "ate lunch with their friends and dinner with their ancestors in paradise." The plague was at its worst between 1347 and 1352, when it killed 25 million people in Europe, or about one-third of the continent's population at the time. Outbreaks of the disease continued for the next few centuries, until better sanitation and medical treatments, along with an understanding of how the disease was spread, helped people control it.

near an important seaport in Ireland. The admiral needed to visit the estate and get to know the local landholders and officials. He decided to send his son to Ireland to fulfill these duties.

In January 1666 Penn sailed to Ireland and settled in at Shangarry Castle. He quickly proved to be an excellent manager of the estate. He became friendly with the local nobility, including the Duke of Ormonde, who was King Charles II's representative in Ireland.

Penn's military skills were also tested when an English army garrison in the nearby town of Carrickfergus mutinied. Along with the Duke of Ormonde's son, the Earl of Arran, Penn helped put down the mutiny. He handled himself so well that the duke wrote to

Sir William to tell him that his son should be a professional soldier. Penn enjoyed the attention, and for a while he did not think about the Quakers or his own religious needs. He later admitted that during this time of his life, "the glory of the world overtook me, and I was even ready to give up myself unto it."

PENN REDISCOVERS THE QUAKERS

Penn's interest in "the glory of the world" did not last very long. In the summer of 1667, he visited the city of Cork and decided to stop at a store to buy some clothes. The store was owned by a Quaker woman whom Penn recognized from his days at Macroom Castle. As the two talked, Penn recalled the Quaker speaker, Thomas Loe, who had come to Macroom and had spoken to the Penns 10 years earlier. Penn told the woman how excited he'd been to hear Loe speak. He said that he would ride 100 miles just to hear the preacher speak again. He was shocked when the woman told him that Loe was in Cork at that very moment and would be speaking at a Quaker meeting the very next day.

Penn attended the meeting. He must have seemed out of place in his fancy clothes because everyone else at the meeting was dressed very plainly, but the Quakers made him feel welcome. Then Loe rose to speak, and said, "There is a Faith that overcometh the world, and there is a Faith that is overcome by the world." The words went straight to Penn's heart, and he realized he had found the answer he'd been seeking all of his life.

Penn began attending Quaker meetings regularly, and in 1667 he officially joined the faith. He knew that his decision was a dangerous one, for Quakers were persecuted in Ireland just as they were in England. It did not take long for Penn's convictions to get him into trouble.

JAIL—AND WORSE

On September 3, 1667, Penn attended a Quaker meeting in Cork. As the meeting started, an English soldier burst into the room, intent on causing trouble. Penn was furious. He jumped up and grabbed the soldier, dragging him toward a flight of steps. Fortunately for them both, a group of Quakers hurried over and stopped Penn before he could throw the soldier down the stairs. They reminded Penn that the Quakers believed in nonviolence.

Penn calmed down and let the soldier go, but it wasn't long before the soldier returned with the local police. Penn and 18 other Quakers at the meeting were arrested and brought to court.

Penn and his friends appeared before Christopher Rye, who was the mayor of Cork and acted as judge that day. Rye recognized Penn as the son of Sir William and an important young gentleman. He could not believe that Penn would be a part of the rebellious Quakers. Clearly there was some mistake. Rye offered to let Penn go. Penn refused and told the mayor that he was, indeed, a member of the Society of Friends, as the Quakers were also called. "Whether you think it or not, I am a Quaker and if you send my friends to jail, I am willing to go with them." Rye immediately threw Penn and his fellow Quakers into jail.

Penn might have been willing to go to jail for his beliefs, but he didn't think it was fair that he or any of the Quakers had been imprisoned. While he was in Cork's prison, he wrote a letter to Lord Orrery, a longtime friend of his father and an important English lord in Ireland. Penn wrote that imprisoning Quakers was unjust because they were not traitors who threatened the government, but rather peaceful people who just wanted to praise God in their own way. Penn also wrote that there was no better way to improve a country than to allow its people "freedom in all things relating to conscience."

Lord Orrery was moved by Penn's letter, and Penn and the other Quakers were soon released from jail. However, Penn's father found out what had happened and he was furious. He wrote to Penn and demanded that he come back to London. Penn ignored this letter, but when his father wrote to him a second time with even firmer instructions, Penn reluctantly returned home. Sir William and his son had a long talk, during which Penn refused to take off his hat as a sign of respect and also used the terms "thee" and "thou" in the Quaker manner of using simple forms of address to anyone, no matter his or her rank in society.

Sir William could not understand why his son had joined the Society of Friends. He told Penn that his religion could destroy everything they had worked so hard for because Penn could not be a Quaker and still achieve a high position in the government. Penn refused to give up his beliefs. His father offered a compromise, saying Penn could use "thee" and "thou" to address anyone he wanted, except for the admiral himself, the king, and the king's brother, the Duke of York. He also insisted that Penn remove his hat for those three people as well. Once again, Penn refused. His father had no choice but to accept his son's decision.

Penn remained in London and became even more active in the Quaker religion. He attended meetings and also wrote letters and tracts, or documents supporting religious positions and beliefs. Penn's father had had enough. He kicked Penn out of the house and told him that he would give his son's inheritance "to someone that pleased him better." For the next few months, Penn lived with other Quakers. Finally free of his father's control, he became one of the most active Quakers in England. He wrote many tracts and also visited several powerful noblemen to argue that persecuting Quakers was immoral.

THE TOWER

In 1668 Penn wrote a pamphlet called *The Sandy Foundation Shaken*. Some of the things he wrote seemed to contradict the basic beliefs

This is a modern photograph of the attic cell in which William Penn was imprisoned in the Tower of London. It was here that he wrote the famous work *No Cross, No Crown*.

of the Anglican Church. The bishop of London became very angry when he read the pamphlet and had Penn arrested and charged with heresy, or speaking against the faith. Penn was imprisoned in the Tower of London.

For the next eight months, Penn lived in a tiny cell under the roof of the tower. His cell was freezing in the winter and as hot as a furnace in the summer. There wasn't much to eat, and the food he was given was poor and sometimes rotten. Penn was not allowed to communicate with anyone. The only message he received was that the bishop would set him free if he recanted, or took back, what he had written. If he didn't, the bishop warned, Penn would stay in prison for the rest of his life. Penn refused to recant and deny his beliefs. "My prison shall be my grave before I will budge [an inch], for I owe my conscience to no mortal man," he wrote to the bishop.

One of the few things Penn was allowed to do in prison was write. He used his time in the tower to write another pamphlet called *No Cross, No Crown*, which would become one of his most famous works. In this pamphlet, Penn explained the Quaker beliefs in detail.

Of course, Sir William knew that his son was imprisoned in the Tower of London, where he himself had been held years earlier after Oliver Cromwell had accused him of treason. Although he would never agree with Penn's beliefs, the older man admired his son for standing up for what he believed. In January 1669, Sir William wrote a new will that stated Penn would inherit the gold chain and medal Cromwell had given to him, as well as most of the estate. He also asked the king to help his son.

King Charles II sent his own personal chaplain, Dr. Edward Stillingfleet, to visit Penn in prison. After many conversations, Penn agreed to write another pamphlet that expressed his beliefs more clearly than he had done in *The Sandy Foundation Shaken.*

In this new pamphlet, Penn clarified his beliefs and made it clear that he had never intended to attack the Anglican Church. Dr. Stillingfleet read the pamphlet and decided that Penn had not committed heresy after all. After the chaplain spoke to Charles II, the king signed an order that set Penn free. Penn walked out of the tower on July 28, 1669, after almost nine months in prison. He was safe for now, but his days in prison were not over.

5

A Courtroom Triumph

After Penn's release from prison, Sir William asked his son to return to Ireland. Penn arrived at Shangarry in October 1669 and set about taking care of his father's affairs. He also discovered that many Irish Quakers were imprisoned under horrifying conditions in Cork's prison. Penn spent months talking to officials in an effort to get the Quakers freed. Finally, in July 1670, the government freed all of the imprisoned Quakers in Ireland.

Just a few weeks later, Penn was on his way back to England. His father had written him a letter asking him to return. "I wish you had . . . done all the business there and that you were here for I find myself to decline." Penn also received an alarming letter from his mother that described just how sick his father was and warned that "the doctor had given over and had said that the fall of the leaf would put him hard to it, and that if not then the first of the winter would carry him away." Sir William knew he was dying and he wanted his son to come home.

A JURY REBELS

Penn might have returned to England to be with his dying father, but that didn't stop him from continuing to preach his Quaker faith. These actions had become increasingly dangerous. King Charles II's mother had been Catholic, and Parliament was afraid that the king might try to reestablish Catholicism as the national church of England. To prevent this, Parliament passed the Conventicle Act in 1664, which prohibited anyone over the age of 16 from meeting in public to practice any religion other than Anglicanism. Most Catholics and members of other religions got around this law by meeting in private, but Quakers firmly believed that they had a moral obligation to practice their faith in public. In the years between 1664 and Penn's arrival home in 1670, many Quakers tested the act by allowing themselves to be arrested. Penn thought this was an interesting idea and decided to give it a try himself.

Penn announced that he and another Quaker named William Mead would hold a religious service at a meeting house in London on August 14. When Penn and Mead showed up for the meeting, they found police blocking the doors of the house and a large crowd that was eager to see what would happen next. Since Penn could not get into the meeting house, he began to preach right in the street. The police immediately arrested both Penn and Mead and brought them to a tavern near Newgate Prison. Newgate was notorious for its brutal conditions, and the authorities were probably nervous about imprisoning an admiral's son there. Instead, they hoped to make an example of Penn without treating him too badly.

Penn thought that he would be released in a few days, but he and Mead were held at the tavern for two weeks. Finally, they were brought to the British court at Old Bailey. When the bailiff, or court officer, read out the charges, Penn was surprised to find that instead of being charged with a minor violation of the Conventicle Act, they were being charged with disturbing the peace because a fight had broken out in the crowd during their arrest. Penn and Mead faced a serious charge of "unlawful and tumultuous assembly" and of gathering "with force and arms . . . against the peace of the King, his Crown, and dignity." This was a serious charge. Penn and Mead now faced a trial before a jury of 12 men and could be put to death for treason if they were convicted.

The trial started on September 3, 1670. As Penn and Mead entered the court, the bailiff grabbed their hats. The judge, Sir Samuel Starling, ordered that the Quakers' hats be returned. As soon as Penn and Mead put their hats back on, Sir Starling fined them for wearing hats in court. Penn, who had a good sense of humor, joked that since the judge had ordered that he and Mead put their hats on, the judge was the one who should be fined, not the Quakers.

Penn's sense of humor did not last long. It quickly became

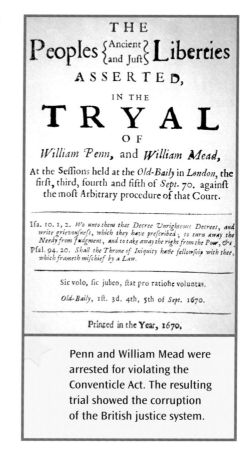

THE

Peoples {Ancient and Juſt} **Liberties**

ASSERTED,

IN THE

TRYAL

OF

William Penn, and *William Mead,*

At the Seſſions held at the *Old-Baily* in *London,* the firſt, third, fourth and fifth of *Sept.* 70. againſt the moſt Arbitrary procedure of that Court.

Iſa. 10. 1, 2. *Wo unto them that Decree Unrighteous Decrees, and write grievouſneſs, which they have preſcribed ; to turn away the Needy from Judgment, And to take away the right from the Poor, &c.*
Pſal. 94. 20. *Shall the Throne of Iniquity have fellowſhip with thee, which frameth miſchief by a Law.*

Sic volo, ſic jubeo, ſtat pro ratiohe voluntas.

Old-Baily, 1ſt. 3d. 4th, 5th of *Sept.* 1670.

Printed in the **Year,** 1670.

Penn and William Mead were arrested for violating the Conventicle Act. The resulting trial showed the corruption of the British justice system.

clear that the trial was a mockery and that Sir Starling was opposed to Penn and Mead and their ideas. Sir Starling allowed only witnesses who spoke against the Society of Friends, and he would not allow Penn and Mead to call witnesses of their own. He even insulted Sir William. Despite the unfair treatment, Penn was able to speak. He told the jurors that the trial threatened the rights of all Englishmen and that the law he was accused of breaking should not be a law at all. Sir Starling and the other court officers became so angry that they ordered Penn to be locked in a portable cell called a bail-dock. As he left the courtroom, Penn called to the crowd, "Is this justice or true judgment? Must I . . . be taken away because I plead for the fundamental laws of England?"

The jury was moved by Penn's eloquent speeches and believed that he was being tried unfairly and that he had not broken any laws. As was common in that time, the judge ordered the jury to find Penn and Mead guilty. However, the jury could not bring themselves to do this. After a short deliberation, the jury announced that it had found Mead innocent and that Penn was guilty only of speaking in the street, which was not a crime.

Sir Samuel Starling was furious. He demanded that the jurors change their verdict and find both men guilty of insurrection or unlawful assembly. If the jurors did not change their verdict, the judge said they would be locked up without food or water. "We will have a verdict, by the help of God or you shall starve for it," he threatened.

Penn was very angry when he heard the judge's threats. He shouted to the courtroom, "It is intolerable that my jury should be thus menaced; their verdict should be free and not compelled. Is this according to fundamental law? Are not they my proper judges the Great Charter of England? What hope is there for ever having justice done when juries are threatened and their verdicts rejected?"

NEWGATE PRISON

Newgate Prison was probably built during the twelfth century. After the original jail burned down in the Great Fire of London in 1666, a new prison was built in 1672 near London's Central Criminal Court, which was commonly known as Old Bailey. Newgate was a horrifying place. Prisoners spent most of the day locked in a large room with a pillar in the middle. At night, the prisoners tied hammocks to the pillar to sleep in, although the sickest and weakest prisoners slept on the floor. Many of the prisoners at Newgate were violent and mentally ill, and the jail was notorious for its cruelty and dangerous conditions. There was not enough food or water, and diseases were common. At about the time when Penn was imprisoned there, a jury came to inspect the prison. The jury foreman was so horrified by the conditions that he said, "I did not think there had been so much cruelty in the hearts of Englishmen."

Newgate Prison was also the site of London's public executions, which were held in a square outside the building. Thousands of people came to watch prisoners being hanged until the practice ended in 1868. Newgate Prison was featured in several of Charles Dickens's books, including *Oliver Twist* and *Great Expectations*. The prison was finally torn down in 1902.

Suddenly, it was not Penn and Mead who were on trial; it was the whole English justice system.

The jury refused to issue a new verdict, so they were locked up, just as the judge had threatened. Two days later, the jury foreman announced that they had a new verdict. Sir Starling was pleased . . . until he heard the new verdict. The jury now said that not only was

Mead innocent of all charges, Penn was innocent as well. The verdict was not really "new" at all. Furious, Sir Starling sent Penn, Mead, and all twelve jurors to Newgate Prison.

Although eight of the jurors quickly paid fines to win their release from Newgate, Penn, Mead, the jury foreman, and three other jurors did not. Penn's father offered to pay Penn's fine because he was anxious for his son to come home, but Penn asked him not to. However, Sir William could not abandon his son, and he did pay his fines, as well as the fines of William Mead. The four jurors, however, remained in Newgate's overcrowded, filthy, and brutal conditions for two months while their case was appealed to a higher court. Finally, the Lord Chief Justice of England ruled that Sir Starling was wrong to try to force the jury to issue a guilty verdict. The Lord Chief Justice said what the judge had done was against the law, and that English juries had to be able to work without any tampering or influence from the judge or other court officials. By refusing to give in, Penn, Mead, and the jurors created an important precedent and changed English law. This same right of law was also used in the English colonies.

A GREAT SORROW

Penn returned home in mid-September. He did not have much time to enjoy his victory because his father was gravely ill. Sir William worried about his oldest son until the end. Before he died, he sent a message to King Charles II and the Duke of York, asking them to protect his son in the years ahead. The royal brothers promised the admiral that they would protect Penn, even though his Quaker religion could mean that Penn could lose his lands, his freedom, and even his life.

Sir William Penn had thought a lot about his son's choices in life and he finally came to accept them. Before he died, Sir William told Penn, "Let nothing in this world tempt you to wrong your

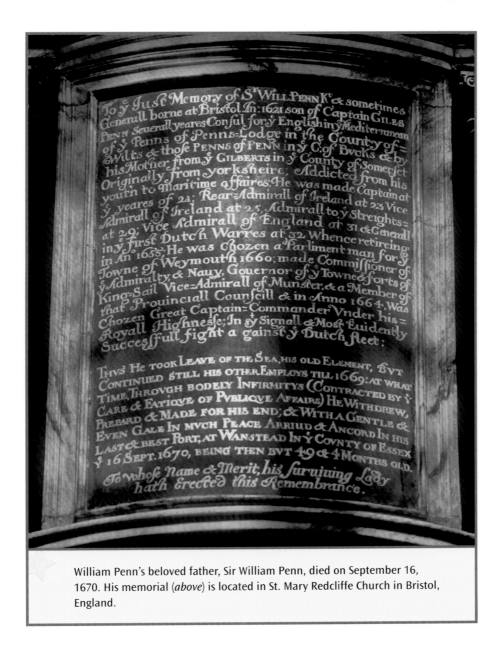

To ȳ Iusṫ Memory of Sᵗ Will. Penn Kᵗ & sometimes
Generall borne at Bristol An:1621 son of Captain Giles
Penn seuerall yeares Consul forȳ English inȳ Mediterranean
ofȳ Penns of Penns-Lodge in the County of=
Wilts & thoſe Penns of Penn inȳ Cᵗ of Bucks & by
his Mother from ȳ Gilberts inȳ County of Somerſet
Originally from yorkſheire; Addicted from his
youth to maritime affaires; He was made Captain at
ȳ yeares of 21; Rear=Admirall of Ireland at 23 Vice
Admirall of Ireland at 25; Admirall toȳ Streights=
at 29; Vice Admirall of England at 31 & Generall
inȳ first Dutch Warres at 32. Whence retireing
in Anᵒ 1655. He was Chozen a Parliment man forȳ
Towne of Weymouth 1660; made Commiſſioner of
ȳ Admiralty & Nauy, Gouernor ofȳ Towne & forts of
King-Sail Vice-Admirall of Munſter, & a Member of
that Prouinciall Counſcill & in Anno 1664, was
Chozen Great Captain=Commander Vnder his =
Royall Highneſſe; In ȳ Signall & Moſt Euidently
Succeſſfull fight a gainſt ȳ Dutch fleet:

Thvs He took Leave of the Sea, his old Element, Bvt
Continued still his other Employs till 1669: At what
Time, Throvgh bodely Infirmitys (Contracted by ȳ
Care & Fatiqve of Pvblicqve Affairs) He Withdrew,
Prepard & Made for his end; & With a Gentle &
Even Gale In mvch Peace Arrivd & Ancord In his
Last & best Port, at Wanstead Inȳ Covnty of Essex
ȳ 16 Sept. 1670, being then bvt 49 & 4 Months old.

To whoſe Name & Merit; his ſuruiuing Lady
hath Erected this Remembrance.

William Penn's beloved father, Sir William Penn, died on September 16, 1670. His memorial (*above*) is located in St. Mary Redcliffe Church in Bristol, England.

conscience. I charge you do nothing against your conscience. Whatever you design to do, lay it justly, and time it seasonably; for that
gives security and dispatch. . . . Son William, if you and your friends

keep to your plain way of preaching and keep to your plain way of living, you will make an end of the priests to the end of the world."

Sir William Penn died on September 16, 1670. He was 49 years old. In his will, Sir William left almost everything to his oldest son. Penn inherited lands in England and Ireland that earned about 1,500 pounds a year, which was a huge fortune at that time. Penn also inherited the responsibilities of running his new estates.

Penn's inheritance allowed him to dedicate his life to the Quakers. He traveled throughout England, speaking and writing. He came to the defense of many Quakers who had been thrown into prison for their beliefs and wrote letters to win their freedom. Soon Penn's own freedom would be in danger.

BACK TO PRISON

On February 5, 1671, Penn was speaking at a meeting in London when soldiers came and arrested him for preaching in public. Once again, Penn went to trial and faced his old enemy, Sir Samuel Starling, as well as Sir John Robinson, who had been Penn's jailer during his stay in the Tower of London several years earlier. Both Starling and Robinson were out to get Penn. They asked him to swear an oath that he would never take up arms against the king. Penn refused because he thought it was silly for him to swear such an oath when, as a Quaker, he practiced nonviolence and did not carry any weapons. "Should I swear not to do what is already against my conscience to do?" Penn asked. Because he refused to swear the oath, Penn was sent back to Newgate Prison. Although he had the money to pay his fines and win his release, Penn refused to do so. He would remain at Newgate until late July, after spending almost six months in the horrors of what he called a "common stinking jail."

After Penn's release, he hurried to get back to his normal life. One of the first things Penn did was go to visit a young Quaker woman named Gulielma Springett, who was called Guli. Penn and Guli had fallen in love and courted for many years. Finally, in 1672, the couple married. Penn called their marriage "a match of Providence's making" and referred to Guli as "the joy of my life" and his "love and delight."

Over the next few years, Penn continued to travel around England and also journeyed to Germany and the Netherlands. Penn preached the Quaker faith and met with the leaders of other religious groups. He returned home whenever he could to be with his wife. The couple dreamed of having a family, but their first three children died in infancy, which was common in those days. Finally, in 1675, Guli gave birth to a healthy son they named Springett. The birth of his first child was only one of the changes Penn and his family would face in the years to come.

6

A New Colony

Penn spent much of his time working to free imprisoned Quakers. It was common for his friends to be sent to prison for preaching and other offenses, and Penn often traveled to help them. During his travels, Penn began to hear stories about new British colonies across the Atlantic Ocean in North America. Quakers who had visited these colonies spoke of the religious freedom they found there, as well as the fertile lands and new opportunities. Penn began to wonder if moving to one of these colonies might be the best way for him to help his fellow Quakers.

QUAKERS IN THE NEW WORLD

At first, Penn resisted the idea of starting a Quaker colony in North America. He wanted to change things in

England and make life better for the religious nonconformists in his homeland. However, as things became more difficult in England, Penn began to wonder if he could ever really change the situation there. Penn wrote that if the British government gave freedom of religion and speech to its citizens and Englishmen were allowed "their own consciences," that "their edge would be taken off, their blood would be sweetened by mercy and truth" and everyone could live in "peace, plenty, and safety."

However, England's rulers were selfish and seemed to care only about gaining power for themselves and hurting anyone who did not share their beliefs. In 1680 Penn said "There is no hope in England." He also said that preaching the idea of freedom of conscience to the English was like trying to play music to charm a deaf snake.

As Penn heard more about the New World, he began to change his mind. Several colonies based on religious freedom had already been set up in North America. The colony of Massachusetts was started by the Puritans. Lord Baltimore had been given the colony of Maryland as a refuge for Catholics.

Even George Fox, the co-founder of the Quaker religion, believed that there was a place in the New World for Quakers. Penn attended many meetings with Fox and often heard the older man speak of the growing number of Quakers living in the New World.

PENN AND NEW JERSEY

In 1676 Penn got his first chance to become involved with the British colonies in North America. At that time, the colony of New Jersey was divided into two parts. Two Quaker colonists living in West Jersey had a dispute over some land there. Because Quakers did not use the courts to settle legal arguments, they needed an arbitrator to settle the case. Because of his legal studies and experience managing his father's estate in Ireland, they wrote to Penn and asked him to do

Members of the Society of Friends founded the town of Burlington, New Jersey. The first Friends' meeting house in Burlington is shown above.

the job. Penn quickly settled the dispute. The Quakers in West Jersey were so pleased with his work that they asked Penn to work with them to set up a plan of government.

Penn and two Quaker leaders soon came up with a plan that was unlike anything ever seen before. The plan was called the Charter or Fundamental Laws of West New Jersey, and it listed all the rights and privileges the colonists would hold. Unlike England's laws, the new colony would allow freedom of speech, freedom of religion, and a fair justice system for all citizens. The document also stated that the rulers "put the power in the people." The Concessions and Agreements also said that Native Americans would be treated the same way as the colonists, which was not noted in any other colony's laws.

Penn also wrote a pamphlet called *The Description of West New Jersey* that promoted the colony's fertile soil, pleasant climate, plentiful fish and animals, and areas of freshwater. This pamphlet encouraged many settlers to travel to the area and build homes there.

Penn never traveled to West Jersey, but he stayed in contact with the Quaker settlers there, including 230 Quakers who sailed to the colony in 1676. These settlers wrote to Penn and described the houses and businesses they were building after buying land rights from the Native Americans. Members of the Society of Friends also founded the town of Burlington. The colony was thriving.

Penn enjoyed hearing the good news from West Jersey, and he became even more convinced that North America was a place where Quakers could live in peace and freedom. However, West Jersey was a small area (it would later join with the rest of New Jersey to form one colony). There was not enough room there for all the Quakers who wanted to leave England and start a new life. Penn needed to come up with something bigger, but he wasn't sure what that place would be yet.

BUSY YEARS

The years between 1677 and 1680 were busy ones for Penn, managing his estates and business dealings. Penn also spent time with his family in their new home at Worminghurst, a country estate near London. In 1677 Penn and Guli were blessed with a daughter they named Laetitia. Their second son, William Jr., was born in 1680.

Penn traveled all over Europe during these years. He visited all the corners of England, as well as Germany and the Netherlands, looking for new converts to his faith and spreading the word about the Quakers. Although Penn did win some new followers for his religion, most people were more interested in hearing about a potential new colony in North America. Penn realized there were a lot of

HOW COLONIES GOT THEIR NAMES

Most of the British colonies in North America were named in honor of British royalty. New York got its name from the Duke of York, King Charles II's brother, James. Virginia was named after Queen Elizabeth I, who was known as the Virgin Queen because she never married. Georgia was named after King George II, while Maryland honored King Charles I's wife, Henrietta Maria, who was called Mary. North and South Carolina were named after King Charles II himself. Other colonies, such as Massachusetts and Connecticut, got their names from Native American tribes.

people who were willing to give up everything to start a new life in the New World.

Penn also kept busy writing. By the time he was 40 years old, he had published more than 50 books and pamphlets about the Quakers and their beliefs.

PENN GETS HIS WISH

Penn felt the time was right to start his own colony. However, he faced a difficult problem. Land grants in the New World could only be given by the king. Although Penn was friendly with King Charles II and his brother, the Duke of York, he wasn't powerful enough to expect a land grant. Even worse, he was a Quaker who had been to prison several times. It didn't seem likely that the king would give Penn the rights to valuable land in the New World.

Once again, Penn's father managed to come to the rescue, even though Sir William had been dead for ten years. King Charles II was always desperate for money, and many years earlier, Sir William had lent him 16,000 pounds, which was a huge sum. Penn knew that King Charles II would never be able to pay back such a large amount, but he had an idea for another way the king could settle the debt. Penn asked the king to grant him land for a colony in the New World in place of paying back the debt. Penn had a specific area of land in mind. He knew there was a large tract of forest between the colonies of Maryland and New York. On June 1, 1680, Penn made a formal written request to Charles II, asking for the land. In exchange, Penn would forgive the debt.

It took nine months for Penn's request to make its way through government and legal channels. King Charles II liked the idea. Giving Penn the land would relieve him of the burden of owing a debt he could never repay. Charles also liked the idea of honoring Penn's father, who had given so much service to the crown. When the king finally issued the charter, he wrote that he had given Penn the land "in the memorie of his late father."

There was probably another reason that Charles II was so agreeable to Penn's idea. He knew that if he gave the Quakers a large tract of land in North America, many of the most troublesome people in England would leave the country for the New World, and the king wouldn't have to bother with them anymore. Penn believed that this was the real reason the king agreed to the deal. Years later, he wrote a letter to a friend and stated, "The government at home was glad to be rid of us at so cheap a rate." Charles II may also have wanted to protect his friend from the persecution of Quakers and other nonconformists that was going on in England at the time.

Finally, after months of waiting, King Charles II signed the charter on March 4, 1681. The charter gave Penn 45,000 square miles (116,550 square kilometers) of land west of the Delaware River. This included the land around the river, which gave Penn an outlet to the

William Penn receives the Charter of Pennsylvania from King Charles II of England. King Charles signed the charter on March 4, 1681.

Atlantic Ocean and a vital trade route. It was the largest territory ever owned by a private citizen. Penn owned everything there: the land, the forests, the wild animals, and any gems or minerals that might be found in the area. Penn could make laws and set up the colony's government any way he wanted to, and he had the right to grant religious tolerance to all Christians. In exchange, Penn had to pay King Charles II "two Beaver Skins to bee delivered att our Castle of Windsor, on the first day of January in every yeare; and also the fifth parte of all Gold and silver Oare."

The king had one more demand to make of Penn. He wanted the colony to be named after Penn's father. King Charles II insisted that the colony be named "Pennsylvania." The name combined Penn's name with the Latin word *sylvania*, which meant "woods," so the colony's name would mean Penn's woods.

Penn hated this idea. He was a modest man and feared that people would think he had named the colony after himself, saying that naming the colony Pennsylvania "should be looked on as a vanity in me." He asked the king to name the colony simply "Sylvania," or "New Wales." King Charles II refused, and Penn finally gave in "as a respect in the King, and to my father." His new colony would be known as Pennsylvania. Penn might not have been pleased with the name, but he was thrilled to finally have a place of his own. Penn later wrote to a friend that acquiring Pennsylvania was "a clear and just thing and God will, I believe, bless it and make it the seed of a nation."

Penn did get to choose the name of his colony's capital, however. He settled on "Philadelphia," which combined two Greek words: *philos*, meaning "love," and *adelphos*, meaning "brother." Penn's capital city would be known as the City of Brotherly Love.

7

Planning Pennsylvania

Penn had his charter and his colony, but there was still a great deal of work to do before anyone would travel to his new lands. It would be two years before Penn even saw the colony that bore his name.

ADVERTISING PENNSYLVANIA

The first thing Penn had to do was get people to come to his new colony. Penn published a pamphlet describing Pennsylvania. The pamphlet told of the land's natural beauty, going into great detail. Penn had never been there to see any of the area for himself, but he noted that he had checked his manuscript with "Traders, Planters, and Shipmasters that know those Parts," and that he had "foreborne allurement and writt truth." Penn gave his work a descriptive title: *Some Account of the Province of Pennsylvania in America, Lately Granted under the Great Seal of England to William Penn, Made Publick for the Information of such as are or may be disposed to Transport themselves or Servants into those Parts.*

Penn also made it clear that he would run the colony with religious freedom as the main rule. He called Pennsylvania a "Holy Experiment," and believed that God had called on him to set up the colony. He wrote, "God had not cast my Lott here but for a service to his Truth, and I know his hand was and is in it." Penn also promised to extend freedom to everyone, not just Quakers or even Christians. He wrote that Pennsylvania would be "a free Colony for all Mankind that should go hither." Penn also wanted his colony to be "an example to the nations" and prove to everyone that people could live in peace if they just respected one another.

Penn also saw Pennsylvania as a chance for him to gain monetary wealth. Despite the large estate his father had left him, Penn lived extravagantly and had many debts. He believed that he could raise a lot of money by selling land

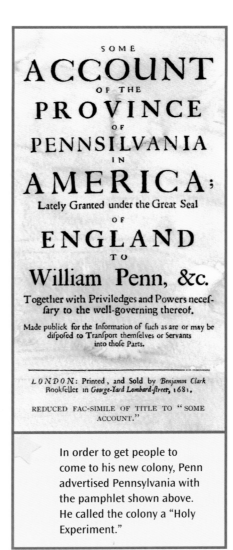

SOME
ACCOUNT
OF THE
PROVINCE
OF
PENNSILVANIA
IN
AMERICA;
Lately Granted under the Great Seal
OF
ENGLAND
TO
William Penn, &c.

Together with Priviledges and Powers necessary to the well-governing thereof.

Made publick for the Information of such as are or may be disposed to Transport themselves or Servants into those Parts.

LONDON: Printed, and Sold by *Benjamin Clark* Bookseller in *George-Yard Lombard-street,* 1681.

REDUCED FAC-SIMILE OF TITLE TO "SOME ACCOUNT."

In order to get people to come to his new colony, Penn advertised Pennsylvania with the pamphlet shown above. He called the colony a "Holy Experiment."

rights in his new colony. Along with his pamphlets, he provided a list of prices for buying land as well as for passage by ship to North America. Five thousand acres cost 100 pounds plus a yearly rent of one shilling per hundred acres. He told Robert Turner, his representative in Ireland, that "though I desire to extend religious freedom, yet I want some recompense for my trouble."

Penn also made allowances for settlers who could not afford to buy land right away but who would rent instead. He wrote, "To [those] that take up land upon rent, they shall have liberty so to do, paying yearly one penny per acre, not exceeding two hundred acres." Penn also allowed for servants to come with their masters, writing "to . . . servants that are carried over, fifty acres shall be allowed to the master for every head, and fifty acres to every servant when their time is expired."

Penn did not limit his advertising to Quakers in England. He sent Robert Turner to Ireland to promote Pennsylvania to the Quakers in that country, and also wrote to Quakers he knew in Germany, Scotland, France, and the Netherlands. Slowly the word spread, and Quakers began to sign up for this new venture. By July, groups of Quakers were setting out across the Atlantic Ocean to their new home.

MAKING FRIENDS

Potential settlers were not the only people Penn wrote letters to. He also contacted the people already living in Pennsylvania. There were about 2,000 European settlers living along the Delaware River in the colony. Penn sent his cousin, William Markham, to Pennsylvania with a letter for those settlers. In it, he promised that they would be able to keep their lands. "My Friends: I hope you will not be troubled with your change," he wrote. "You are now fixt, at the mercy of no Governor that comes to make his fortune great. You shall be governed by laws of your own making and live a free people. I shall not usurp the right of any, or oppress his person. . . . In short, whatever . . . free men can reasonably desire for the security and improvement of their own happiness, I shall heartily comply with."

In addition to his residents, Penn also wrote to the leaders of the other colonies in America. He wanted to make sure that he and his settlers would be welcomed in their new home. Penn was especially concerned about relations with Lord Baltimore, who owned the neighboring colony of Maryland. Penn and Lord Baltimore had already had a dispute over the boundary lines around Chesapeake Bay and the Delaware River and how far north the border between the two colonies extended. Their dispute would eventually go to court in England for resolution. Penn did his best to make sure his settlers would not have any problems as they settled on the land they had bought from Penn.

Perhaps most important, Penn wrote to Native American tribes in Pennsylvania. While many colonial leaders treated Native Americans as a nuisance to be abused, taken advantage of, and eventually gotten rid of, Penn was determined to respect the natives and live in peace with them. His letter made it clear that he saw the Native Americans as equals to the Europeans. Penn wrote to the Delaware, Susquehannock, and Shawnee Indians, "My Friends, There is one great God and power that hath made the world and all things therein, to whom you and I must one day give an account, for all that we do in the world."

THE FIRST FRAME

Penn had one more vital task to accomplish before he left for Pennsylvania. He had to write a constitution that described the laws of his new colony. During the summer of 1681, Penn met with a group of settlers who had bought land in the new colony but hadn't left

TRANSATLANTIC TRAVEL

Today a traveler can fly from Europe to North America in just a few hours, but things were very different during the 1600s. In those days, the only way across the Atlantic Ocean was by ship, and the journey took several months. Conditions were extremely difficult. The ships of those times were small and made of wood, and they were tossed around violently by the ocean's waves, especially during a storm. Seasickness was common, and the passengers were crowded closely together, making it easy for disease to spread. It was not unusual for a number of passengers to die during the voyage. About 30 passengers died of smallpox during Penn's journey to America in 1682. Passengers also had to share the space with the goods they were bringing, which could include animals, such as goats, horses, and chickens. People spent most of their time below deck in quarters that were dark, damp, and almost airless. The type of food available on board was also limited to a type of biscuit called hardtack, salted or smoked meats, and fruits, and the food was always in danger of being infested with insects, mice, or rats. By the time settlers arrived in the New World, they had already survived a difficult and dangerous experience.

for their new homes yet. Penn also asked many of Europe's leading thinkers and political experts for advice. Finally, in July 1682, Pennsylvania's constitution was ready. Penn called the document "the First Frame." The document was based on the charter Penn had helped create for West Jersey. It had a preface and 24 sections that spelled out exactly how the new colony would be governed.

The First Frame stated that the head of the colony would be a governor, either Penn himself or someone he appointed to the post.

The governor would not have complete power, however. Instead, he would work with an elected council of 72 members and an elected general assembly that could number up to 500 members. Nothing could become law unless the governor, the council, and the general assembly all agreed to it. The three bodies would also have to agree on how the business of the colony would run.

Penn's constitution also spelled out important rules of religious freedom. Anyone who held public office had to be a Christian, but anyone who believed in God could live in the colony, no matter what religion he or she followed, or even if the person did not follow any particular religion at all. No one would ever be persecuted for their religious beliefs or how they worshiped, nor would they be forced to attend any religious gatherings if they did not want to. To Penn, religious freedom was the most important goal of his new society. In a letter to a friend, he said, "I abhor two principles in religión, and pity those that own them. The first is obedience upon authority without conviction; and the other the destroying of them that differ from me for God's sake."

The First Frame also gave the right to vote to every man who owned property and provided for free elections. Voters had to approve all taxes. Penn also wrote at length about the rights of prisoners. The First Frame stated that government officials or judges could not interfere in jury trials. There were only two crimes that were punishable by death: treason and murder. Other colonies had many more crimes that were punished by death. Penn also planned for prisons to be more than a place where people were locked up and forgotten while they suffered horrible abuses. Instead, Penn wanted the colony's prisons to provide workshops to teach prisoners a trade so they could have a better and more productive life when they were released.

The First Frame also said that all children over the age of 12 had to be taught a trade or a skill. The document even protected the rights of the colony's Native Americans and extended the right for a jury trial to these people as well. Finally, the First Frame said that the constitution could be amended, or changed, if the need arose. This provision actually gave away some of Penn's power and put changes in government in the hands of the citizens. This was very different from the government that the Puritans had set up in the Massachusetts colony. Massachusetts's legal code was based on biblical concepts and written as a covenant with God that could never be changed. Penn's vision was more relaxed and allowed for the development of social changes. Many historians view this as one of Penn's most important achievements. A century later, the French writer Voltaire credited Penn with creating "that golden age of which men talk and which probably has never existed anywhere except in Pennsylvania."

At that time, no other government guaranteed so many rights and freedoms for its citizens. Historian Brent Barksdale noted that "The government that William Penn established in 1682 was far more liberal and responsible to the people than any antecedent or contemporary form on earth."

Many of the ideas Penn included in his constitution would later appear in the Declaration of Independence and become part of the United States Constitution when the colonies banded together and declared their independence from England almost a century later. Penn's ideas were truly ahead of their time.

8

The Business of Running a Colony

Several hundred settlers had already traveled to Pennsylvania by the middle of 1682. Penn had too much business in England to finish in time to journey with the earlier settlers, but in August 1682, he was finally able to visit his new land. Penn's wife, Guli, and their three children stayed behind, and Penn wrote fond letters to each of them before he left. Then Penn headed off to the New World.

PENN'S ARRIVAL

After a long journey across the Atlantic, Penn's ship, *Welcome*, docked in New Castle, Pennsylvania, on October 27, 1682. New Castle was a small community that had been built by Dutch settlers years earlier. Many of the colony's 3,000 settlers came to New Castle to greet Penn, among them groups of Native Americans. Penn was pleased at his reception.

Penn spent his first night in Pennsylvania sleeping aboard the ship. The next morning, he received an official welcome from William Markham and other officials of the new colony. In a short ceremony, Penn received a key to the fort at New Castle, along with a clump of earth with a twig growing in it and a bowl of water from the Delaware River as symbols of the land Penn owned.

After the ceremony, Penn traveled up the Delaware River. He visited several small communities along the way, meeting Quakers, settlers that had come to the area from Sweden before England took possession of the territory, and bands of Native Americans.

As he journeyed up the river, Penn must have been pleased with what he saw. The river was lined with thick forests of beech, hickory, walnut, oak, and poplar trees. Penn glimpsed deer, wild turkeys, rabbits, and more animals through the trees, as well as flocks of ducks on the water. Clearly this was a land of plenty.

THE CITY OF BROTHERLY LOVE

Penn's next stop was the capital city, Philadelphia, a place that Penn had taken special care in planning. Penn had spent most of his life in the dirty, twisted, overcrowded streets of London, and he envisioned something very different for Philadelphia. That city's streets were broad and straight and crossed each other at right angles. Lots were large so they could be planted with trees and flowers, creating small parks within the city. Penn called Philadelphia "a green country town." It was the first time anyone had planned out a city before it was built, and Philadelphia's layout would be copied by other towns in the New World.

Penn landed in New Castle, Pennsylvania, on October 27, 1682. He was greeted by many settlers as well as local Native Americans.

William Markham, who had traveled to Pennsylvania before Penn to oversee the colony, had chosen the site of the colony's new capital. Markham decided Philadelphia would be located on a bluff near the Delaware River, at a spot where a small creek emptied into the river, creating a natural harbor. The site was dry and free of mosquitoes and other insects that could spread disease. Markham knew the area would be healthy for its residents. Construction started even before Penn left England, and he was pleased with the progress that had been made.

NATIVE AMERICANS IN PENNSYLVANIA

Native Americans had lived in Pennsylvania for many years before William Penn arrived in the late 1600s. At the time of Penn's arrival, the most powerful tribe in the area was the Lenape, also known as the Leni Lenape. This tribe was part of the Algonquian-speaking nation and lived along the Delaware River. Over time, smaller tribes, including the Nanticokes, the Connoys, and the Mahicans, were driven from their homes in New York by the Iroquois and other Native American tribes. They fled to Pennsylvania, where they joined the Lenape and became part of their nation. The Susquehannocks were another powerful Algonquian-speaking tribe. These natives lived along the Susquehanna River in Pennsylvania and also in Maryland.

Unfortunately, many Native Americans were killed by European settlers. Thousands more died from diseases they caught from Europeans. Today, some descendants of the Native American tribes still live in Pennsylvania, but the state has one of the lowest Native American populations in the United States.

Penn also took special attention to the building of his manor house, which he named Pennsbury. After he left Philadelphia, Penn and his companions sailed about 24 miles (38 km) north to the site of his estate. Markham had purchased a large tract of land from the Native Americans, and Penn's manor house may already have been under construction when he arrived there in the fall of 1682. When it was completed, Pennsbury was a large, three-story house made of red brick. It had wide windows that let in plenty of light and fresh air. A tree-lined path led from the front of the house down to the Delaware River, and a garden sat behind the house. The estate also included a bakehouse, an office, and a large barn.

GETTING DOWN TO BUSINESS

After viewing Pennsbury, Penn traveled back to Philadelphia, where he would live until his manor house was finished. Once he settled in, Penn got right to work, and there was much to do. He had to assign land to settlers and meet with them to make sure everyone was being treated fairly. Penn also met with elected officials to make sure the government was running properly. In November he traveled to the colonies of New York and East Jersey to meet with their leaders.

One of Penn's most important goals in those early days was to meet with Native Americans. From the very beginning, Penn had been determined to treat the natives with dignity and respect. Penn had written a letter to the Native Americans, which was delivered by three of his commissioners when they traveled to the colony to lay out the site for Philadelphia. In this letter, Penn told the Native Americans that he did not wish "to enjoy the great province his king had given him without the Indians' consent." Penn assured the natives that, although other Englishmen had treated them unfairly, "I am not such a man, as is well known in my own country, I have a great love and regard for you, and I desire to win and gain your love and friendship by a kind, just, and peaceable life, and the people I send are all of the same mind, and shall in all things behave them-selves accordingly, and if in anything any shall offend you or your people, you shall have a full and speedy satisfaction."

From his earliest days in the colony, Penn made himself available to the Native Americans, many of whom belonged to a tribe known as the Lenape. Penn met with any native leaders who wanted to talk to him. He visited native settlements, ate with Native Americans, and even joined in their sports and games. Penn had been an excellent runner in his youth and impressed the Native Americans by beating some of them in races. Penn even learned enough of the

Penn was determined to be diplomatic when dealing with Native Americans. He signed a treaty with the Lenape in the area, promising fair treatment.

Lenape language to be able to talk to the natives without needing an interpreter.

Penn knew it was important to have a formal agreement with the Native Americans regarding his ownership of Pennsylvania. In 1683 Penn drew up a land purchase agreement and a peace treaty with the most powerful local tribe, the Lenape. Penn and the Lenape leaders met at Shackamaxon, just north of Philadelphia. Although there are no formal records of this meeting, stories about it have been passed down in both Native American history and in histories told by the settlers' families.

Penn met with the Native Americans under a large elm tree that later came to be known as the Treaty Elm. Representatives of the Susquehannock and Shawnee tribes also attended. Tradition says that Penn wore a blue sash over his clothes to show the natives that he was the highest-ranking chief of his people and to follow a Native American tradition that chiefs wore special decorations to indicate their rank. The Lenape chief called Penn *Onas*, which was the native word for "quill" or "pen." Although no one is sure that their agreement was written down, history says that Penn and the Lenape chief worked out a document called the Great Treaty that spelled out Penn's high regard for the Native Americans and his promises to treat them fairly. Given that the United States has a poor history of keeping its promises to Native Americans, many people say that the Great Treaty was the only agreement between Europeans and Native Americans that was never broken.

BORDER DISPUTE

Penn's dealings with the Native Americans went smoothly, but he was not so fortunate in his other affairs. Even before he left England, Penn had gotten caught up in a border dispute with Lord Baltimore, the leader of the Maryland colony. In order to give Penn a trade route and to link Pennsylvania with the Atlantic Ocean, the Duke of York had sold land along the Delaware River and Chesapeake Bay to Penn as part of the purchase of Pennsylvania. These lands came from Lord Baltimore's holdings, who argued that the Duke of York did not own the lands, so he could not sell them to Penn.

Before Penn left for Pennsylvania, he had authorized his representatives in North America to meet with Lord Baltimore to find a solution to the problem. Discussions did not go well, however, and Lord Baltimore insisted that part of Pennsylvania, including its capital city of Philadelphia, was actually in Maryland's territory, 40 miles (64 km) south of what he considered to be the real border of Pennsylvania. Penn traveled to Maryland to meet directly with Lord Baltimore. He argued that Pennsylvania needed the Delaware River in order to have a trade link with the Atlantic Ocean, but Lord Baltimore refused to give in. The meeting ended with no resolution to the problem.

LEAVING PENNSYLVANIA

Penn worked hard during 1683 and 1684. By the fall of 1683, Philadelphia was doing well, and there were 80 houses already built in the city. Many of these houses were made of brick and were quite elegant for their time. Other areas of the colony were thriving as well. A ship full of settlers arrived from England almost every week. Penn had to help these new residents get settled, which was not an easy task since they had no homes or even cleared land when they arrived. New settlers often camped out in the forest or dug caves into the banks of the river where they lived until they could build crude log cabins or other simple shelters.

Penn also stayed in touch with his family back in England. In 1683 he received word that his wife, Guli, had given birth to a baby girl. Although the baby was healthy at first, sad news came just a few weeks later that the baby had died.

In 1684 Penn received news that Lord Baltimore was on his way to England to resolve the land dispute between Maryland and Pennsylvania directly with the king. Penn knew he needed to talk to the king himself, or he would be at a terrible disadvantage in his arguments with Lord Baltimore. Penn left numerous instructions with his representatives in Pennsylvania so they could run the colony while he was away. Then, in August 1684, Penn boarded a ship and sailed to England. He hoped to return as soon as possible, this time bringing his wife and children with him. Penn had no idea that he would not see Pennsylvania again for 15 years.

9

Problems

Penn returned to an England that was very different than the one he had left just two years earlier. King Charles II was in poor health. Parliament was not in session when Penn arrived, so the government was basically not operating. Nothing could be done about the border dispute between Maryland and Pennsylvania, and Penn would face even more difficulties in the years to come.

ROYAL CHALLENGES

Things had gotten worse for the Quakers since Penn had left. Over the past two years, King Charles II was challenged by Parliament about many aspects of his rule. Instead of compromising, Charles II reacted with violence. He became a tyrant who attacked anyone who might threaten him, including any religious or political non-conformists. Many Quakers were jailed or even executed, meeting houses were destroyed, and "dangerous" books were publicly burned. When Penn returned to England, about 1,400 Quakers were in prison.

Penn found himself in an awkward position. On the one hand, he was friendly with the king and his brother, the Duke of York, and he didn't want to argue with them. At the same time, he had to stand up for the Quakers and try to help those in prison to regain their freedom. Penn knew that by defending the Quakers, he risked jail or even execution.

Penn decided to use his skill at writing to try to solve his problem. He wrote an essay called *True Interest of King and Kingdom*. In it, he advised Charles II to act moderately and warned that he might tear England apart even as he tried to protect her from threats. Instead of publishing his essay, Penn sent it directly to the king.

It is doubtful that King Charles II ever read Penn's essay. On February 1, 1685, the king suffered a massive stroke. Penn wrote a letter to some Quaker friends in Pennsylvania and described what had happened: "About eight next morning, as he sat down to shave, his head twitched both ways . . . and he gave a shriek, and fell as dead." Five days later, Charles II died. His brother, the Duke of York, was now King James II.

Penn hoped that James II would be a more tolerant ruler than his brother had been. At first, Penn's optimism was rewarded. On April 23, 1685, the new king issued a declaration that ended some of the religious persecution. Just one month later, however, a group of noblemen rebelled against James II and tried to take the crown from him. In response to the dissent, James II cracked down on anyone who disagreed with him. Penn was forced to walk a dangerous

Upon the death of King Charles II, his brother James ascended the throne. James II proved to be stricter; Penn gently tried to persuade the king to change his policies.

tightrope, remaining friendly with the king while trying to convince him that his cruel persecutions were morally wrong and dangerous to England.

In the midst of these uncertain times, Penn finally received some good news. The government resolved the border dispute between Maryland and Pennsylvania by splitting the territory along the Delaware River in half. Pennsylvania received the land along the Delaware River, while Maryland received the eastern portion of the territory, an area now known as the Eastern Shore. However, the exact border between Pennsylvania and Maryland would not be decided until many years after both Penn and Lord Baltimore died.

POLITICAL TURMOIL

Penn was eager to return to Pennsylvania once the border dispute was resolved. He heard from his representatives there that arguments had broken out between Quaker and non-Quaker settlers, and that there was immoral behavior going on, especially in Philadelphia's taverns. Penn knew that his enemies in England were also receiving these reports, and he felt a lot of pressure to make his colonists behave better. In a letter to his representatives, Penn begged, "Cannot more friendly and private courses be taken to set matters to rights in an infant province whose steps are . . . watched? For the love of God, me, and the poor country, be not so governmentish; so noisy and open in our disaffections."

However, Penn also felt needed in England, where he could plead the cause of his persecuted Quaker friends and try to convince King James II to change his policies. Penn did manage to win pardons for several of his friends and other people who came to him asking for help. Finally, Penn won a great victory when King James II issued a general pardon in March 1686. The pardon ordered that all religious prisoners be released, freeing more than 1,300 Quakers. Penn was thrilled and called the pardon "something wonderful that God had wrought."

Unfortunately for Penn and King James II, the king went on to suspend other laws against noncomformists, but he did so without Parliament's approval. Soon afterward, he tried to force one of the Protestant colleges at Oxford University to accept a Catholic as its head. When several Anglican bishops complained about this and other actions, James II had them arrested for treason.

Parliament and many English citizens had had enough. When James II and his wife had a baby boy in June 1688, it became clear that the child, who was heir to the throne, would be raised as a Catholic. Until then, most people believed that James's oldest child, a grown daughter from his first marriage named Mary, would inherit the throne. After James II's son was born, a group of the most powerful lords in England invited Charles II's daughter, Mary, and her husband, William of Orange, to accept the throne. Mary and William had been living in the Netherlands, but they accepted the offer.

On November 5, 1688, William of Orange landed in England with an army of 14,000 men. King James was quickly deposed and sent into exile in France. This event became known as the Glorious Revolution. However, this turn of events was less than glorious for Penn. He had always had enemies, and now he fell under suspicion for his friendship with the deposed King James II. William of Orange, who ruled as King William III, did not trust Penn. Although Penn defended himself, the king and queen didn't believe him. In February 1689, they issued a warrant for Penn's arrest on suspicions of high treason.

Penn went into hiding, moving from one house to another. To make matters worse, his beloved wife's health was failing and the couple had buried another child, their four-year-old daughter, named Gulielma after her mother. Although a judicial hearing cleared him of the treason charge in November 1690, Queen Mary charged him with treason again in February 1691, claiming that he was trying to "subvert the government of this kingdom by procuring an invasion of the same by the French."

Once again, Penn went into hiding. In a letter to some Quaker friends, he complained that "men have sworn . . . falsely against me." He also asked some of his influential friends to speak to the king. "Lay my case before him and dispose him to regard me and mine under our present great difficulties. . . . I say, and that truly, that I know of no invasions or insurrections, men, money, or arms." He also asked the king to "allow me to live quietly anywhere, either in this kingdom or in America." Despite his friends' pleas, William and Mary refused to dismiss the charges against Penn. He remained in hiding and on the run.

An even worse blow fell when the crown took over the governorship of Pennsylvania. In October 1692 Pennsylvania was taken away from Penn's control and annexed to the colony of New York. A royal governor was appointed to command the province. The king and queen did not actually take this action to punish Penn, but to protect Pennsylvania in case of a war with France. Since Pennsylvania was ruled by Quakers who believed in nonviolence, they would not fight against France if there was a war, so annexing the colony to New York was a way to keep it defended and safe.

Penn still had friends in high places, and one of them was a philosopher named John Locke. Locke, who was a friend of King William III, brought Penn's case to court and argued that Penn should be pardoned. This time, the king and queen listened. In 1694 the charges against Penn were dropped and he was able to come out of hiding.

Penn quickly returned home to his family, but his homecoming was not a happy one. His wife, Guli, had suffered greatly during

Penn's ordeal, and she was now very ill. Penn spent every moment he could with her, even refusing invitations to speak at Quaker meetings. He was with Guli when she died on February 23, 1694, at the age of 48. Penn was heartbroken at her death. He wrote that "she was not only an excellent wife and mother, but an entire and constant friend . . . an easy mistress and a good neighbor, especially to the poor."

NEW LIFE

Penn was never really the same after Guli's death. Soon afterward, he wrote to his old friend, Robert Turner, "Loving Friend, My extreme great affliction for the decease of my dear wife, makes me unfit to write much. . . . In great peace and sweetness she departed, and to her gain, but our incomparable loss."

Penn spent the winter and spring at home, enjoying time with his oldest son, Springett. He began making public appearances again that summer and received good news when King William and Queen Mary signed a royal decree in August that returned Pennsylvania to his personal possession. The agreement demanded that Penn go back to Pennsylvania to govern it. Penn was agreeable, but he did not want to go alone. He decided to marry again.

In 1695 Penn attended a Quaker meeting and met Hannah Callowhill, a 30-year-old Quaker who had never married. The two quickly became friends, and Penn decided he and Hannah were a good match. On March 5, 1696, the couple married. Unfortunately, just a few weeks later, Penn's beloved son, Springett, died of a respiratory infection at the age of 21. Penn was heartbroken. He wrote, "So ended the life of my dear child and eldest son, much of my comfort and hope . . . in whom I lost all that any father can lose in a child, since he was capable of anything that became a sober young man; my friend and companion, as well as most affectionate and dutiful child."

Hannah Callowhill Penn (1664–1726) was William Penn's second wife. When Penn died, Hannah was given full control of the Pennsylvania colony.

RETURN TO PENNSYLVANIA

Penn spent the next three years putting his affairs in order. Finally, in 1699, he was ready to return to Pennsylvania, the colony he had not seen for 15 years. He and Hannah, accompanied by Penn's daughter Laetitia, sailed across the Atlantic. They arrived in the colony in December 1699. The family settled at Pennsbury, where they would live for the next two years. During this time, Hannah gave birth to a son, John. John was the only one of Penn's children to be born in the New World, and he carried the nickname "the American" for the rest of his life.

Penn's arrival was greeted with great rejoicing. Hundreds of brightly decorated boats surrounded Penn's ship, and the shore was lined with people waving banners and cheering the return of their leader.

Much had changed in the 15 years Penn had been away. He hardly recognized the colony. When he left, there had been just a few thousand people living there, many of them in simple dwellings on the edge of the wilderness. By 1699 Pennsylvania was a prosperous center of commerce and manufacturing. His dream city, Philadelphia, was especially grand. The city now had 10,000 inhabitants and its wide, tree-lined streets were filled with shops and businesses such as weavers, candle makers, carpenters, and food manufacturers. Trade flourished between Pennsylvania and Europe, and the cities and larger towns were filled with the finest English goods, including shoes, tools, and clothing.

Penn was pleased at the state of his colony, but he wanted to make it even better. He was delighted by the religious diversity of Pennsylvania, the residents of which included members of many religions, not just Quakers. He decided to bring the members of different religions in even closer contact by implementing an open

LIFE AT PENNSBURY

Penn and his family lived a very aristocratic life at their estate in Pennsbury. The estate included extravagant gardens that were tended by a large number of servants. Servants also managed the three-story mansion. Dinners were elaborate feasts that included several courses washed down with beer brewed right on the estate. Penn also owned several carriages for travel, pulled by teams of fine horses. To travel down the Delaware River, Penn used a splendid covered barge rowed by six oarsmen. This lifestyle was typical of a man of Penn's importance and social position, but he did not have the money to maintain this way of life without going into debt.

admission to Quaker schools. Every boy and girl under the age of 12 was required to attend school, whether they were members of the Society of Friends or not. In effect, Penn started one of the first public school systems.

Political matters also occupied Penn's attention. He remained on good terms with the Native Americans and negotiated a new treaty with the Susquehannocks soon after his arrival. In 1701 Penn wrote a new constitution called the Charter of Privileges. This document ensured religious freedom for all residents of the colony and remained in effect until 1776, when it was replaced by a new state constitution. The Charter of Privileges later served as a model for the U.S. Constitution.

Penn and his family might have stayed in Pennsylvania, but once again, trouble with England changed their plans. By 1701 war was brewing between England and France. England was once again threatening to take control of Pennsylvania because its Quaker citizens refused to fight. Penn knew his only chance of keeping control of the colony was to return to England. At the same time, his wife, Hannah, and daughter, Laetitia, were also eager to return to the brighter social life available in English society. In 1701 the family returned to England, never to return to the New World.

10

Passing On

Penn faced many problems after his return to England. From personal problems with his son William Jr. to enormous debts and a betrayal by one of his most trusted friends, Penn's last years were difficult and bittersweet for a man who had achieved so much in his life.

FINANCIAL RUIN

For many years, Penn had placed his business affairs and his trust in the hands of a friend named Philip Ford. Over the years, he had signed many documents that Ford gave him, never bothering to read the papers and always believing the explanations Ford gave him as to what the papers were about. In addition, Penn had borrowed money from Ford many years earlier and Ford charged him a very high interest rate without telling Penn what he was doing. Ford also gave Penn documents to sign that turned over property to Ford or demanded payments for transactions that Penn was not even aware of. Neither Penn nor any of his friends knew what Ford was doing, and Penn had known Ford for so long and trusted him so deeply that it's doubtful he would have believed it if anyone had warned him about it.

Penn remained unaware of his friend's deception until he returned to England in 1701. Ford demanded that Penn repay everything he owed—a tremendous fortune of 10,000 pounds. Penn did not have anywhere near that amount. He had poured most of his own wealth into Pennsylvania and never managed to collect most of the rents and other payments that he expected from the sale of his lands. Penn also was not good at managing money and lived well beyond his means, without any real understanding of where his money was going and what income was being earned.

Philip Ford died in 1702, but his claims on Penn did not end. Ford's widow, Bridget, and the Ford family continued to demand that Penn pay his debts. Bridget even demanded ownership of the colony of Pennsylvania and threatened to sell it. Penn owed so much money that he could not support his family, so Hannah and their growing family moved back to live with her father in Bristol.

Penn reviewed his accounts and had some of his Quaker friends go over them. Everyone was shocked to discover that Ford had tricked and cheated Penn. Penn took the Fords to court. He and his friends testified that the Fords had cheated Penn and that he had signed documents without knowing what they were. Penn was confident that he would win. England was now ruled by Queen Anne, who was the younger daughter of Penn's old friend King James II. However, the case dragged on for three years. Things got so bad that in 1708, Penn was arrested and sentenced to debtors' prison. Penn

PHILADELPHIA DURING
THE AMERICAN REVOLUTION

No city was more important than Philadelphia during the American Revolution. At the start of the revolution, Philadelphia was by far the largest city in the colonies, with a population of about 25,000 people. It was also centrally located and in a convenient place for meetings. In 1774 the First Continental Congress was held in Philadelphia, with 56 delegates representing 12 colonies. During the summer of 1776, delegates met again and declared their independence from Great Britain when the Declaration of Independence was first read to the public on July 3, in the streets of Philadelphia. The city was captured by the English early in the war, but the British abandoned the city in 1778 to focus their attention on battles farther north.

did not actually go to prison but was placed under house arrest for nine months because he could not settle his accounts.

Finally, pressure from Queen Anne and from Penn's influential friends forced the Fords to lower their demands. An agreement was reached that had Penn pay 67,000 pounds as a settlement of all his debts to the Fords. This amount was still more than he could pay, but nine of Penn's Quaker friends raised the money and paid off the debt.

With the resolution of the Ford case, Penn was finally able to rejoin his family. He found a home for Hannah and all their children in Ruscombe in the countryside between London and Oxford. Penn spent the next few years corresponding with his representatives in Pennsylvania and also remained active with the Society of Friends.

PERSONAL DIFFICULTIES

The Ford case was not the only problem Penn faced after his return to England. His oldest surviving son, William Jr., called Billy, had married and fathered several children, but he was more interested in drinking, gambling, and partying than he was in supporting his family and going into a respectable business. For many years, Penn had paid most of his son's bills and allowed Billy and his wife and children to live with him. In 1703 Penn decided that what his son needed was some responsibility, so he sent Billy to Pennsylvania to serve as Penn's representative. Billy did not want to go, but his father threatened to stop paying his debts if he didn't, so off Billy went.

Things did not go as well as Penn had hoped they would. In 1704 he received word that Billy had become involved in a tavern brawl. One of Pennsylvania's leading Quakers wrote, "I wish things had been better, or he had never come. He is my greatest affliction, for his soul's and my country's and family's sake." Another colonist told Penn, "I supposed you will have a more ample account by others of the condition this poor Province is brought to by the late revels and disorders which young William Penn and his gang of loose fellows he accompanies with are found in, to the great grief of Friends and others in this place." Penn had no choice but to order Billy to come home.

After he returned to England, Billy continued to disappoint his father by turning his back on the Quaker faith and taking up arms as a soldier. Penn tried his best to support his son and respect his personal freedom, but his writings make it clear that he was very upset at how things turned out. "O Pennsylvania! What hast thou cost me?" he wrote in a letter to a friend. "Above thirty thousand pounds more than I ever got by it, two hazardous and most frightening voyages, my . . . slavery here, and my child's soul almost."

PENN'S LAST YEARS

Penn still faced financial difficulties and had debts to pay. He was also in his late sixties and his health was not as strong as it once was. Penn decided to give up his rights to Pennsylvania. He realized the only way to settle his debts was to sell Pennsylvania back to the crown. For several years, he negotiated with the royal family and its advisors. Finally, in 1712, he accepted an offer from Queen Anne to sell the colony to her for 12,000 pounds paid over four years, with 1,000 pounds payable immediately.

Before the final agreement could be reached, Penn suffered a stroke. On October 4, 1712, Penn was writing a letter to James Logan, one of his representatives in Pennsylvania, when his writing stopped in the middle of the page. His wife, Hannah, finished the letter, writing that Penn had suffered an attack of a "lethargich illness."

Penn's stroke left him partially paralyzed and also affected his mind. He recovered somewhat but he was no longer able to manage his affairs. Because of his inability to conduct business, the sale of Pennsylvania to the crown was stopped. His family would hold the charter to the colony until the American Revolution, when all the colonies became independent states in the United States of America.

Hannah cared for Penn in Bristol for a few months before they returned to London early in 1713. Soon afterward, the family went back to their country home in Ruscombe, where Penn suffered another, more serious stroke. From then on, he was unable to care for himself and he lost most of his memory. He spent much of the next five years in bed, although he sometimes was taken outside to enjoy the sunshine and the beautiful gardens around his house. His friend and fellow Quaker Thomas Story visited Penn and described him as "pretty well in health, and cheerful of disposition, but defective in memory, nor could he deliver his words so

William Penn is buried with his family in the Quaker cemetery at Jordans Friends Meeting House in England.

readily heretofore." Story was upset by Penn's disability and wrote, "When I went to the house I thought myself strong enough to see him in that condition, but when I entered the room and perceived the great defect of his expressions, for want of memory, it greatly bowed my spirit."

Penn's health continued to fail. In late July 1718, he came down with an attack of chills and fever. He died early in the morning of July 30, 1718, at the age of 73. Penn was buried in a graveyard next to a Quaker meeting house called Jordans Friends Meeting House, next to the grave of his first wife, Guli, and the many children who had died before him.

PENN'S LEGACY

William Penn had a huge effect on English politics and law, but his greatest legacy is in the United States. Penn spent only four years in Pennsylvania, but he put his beliefs into action there and changed the path of American history. Penn was a pioneer in cooperating with Native Americans, as well as allowing his colonists to rule themselves and settle disputes peacefully. Penn also set the standard for religious freedom, a standard that was incorporated into the United States government after the colonies joined together to become an independent nation. Without Penn's efforts, the United States might be a very different country today. Although William Penn made his mark on the world more than 300 years ago, he continues to be a symbol of courage and conviction and a man who changed the world.

Chronology

1644	William Penn is born on October 14 in London.
1662	Expelled from Oxford for his nonconformist actions.
1665	Studies law at Lincoln's Inn.
1666	Goes to Ireland to manage his father's estates.

TIMELINE

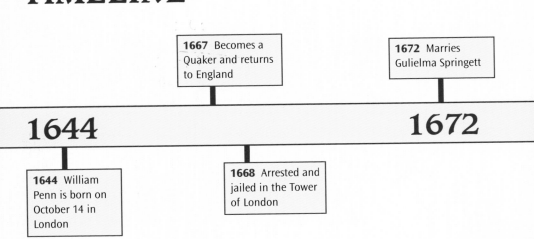

1667 Becomes a Quaker and returns to England

1672 Marries Gulielma Springett

1644

1672

1644 William Penn is born on October 14 in London

1668 Arrested and jailed in the Tower of London

1667	Becomes a Quaker and returns to England.
1668	Arrested and jailed in the Tower of London.
1670	A trial featuring Penn brings about a new legal ruling that juries cannot be punished for their verdicts.
1672	Marries Gulielma Springett.
1676	Arbitrates the boundaries for the colony of West Jersey.
1681	Receives the charter for Pennsylvania.
1682	Arrives in Pennsylvania.
1684	Returns to England to settle a boundary dispute between Pennsylvania and Maryland.
1694	Penn's wife, Gulielma, dies.

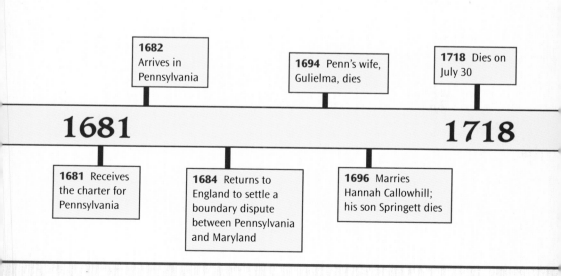

1682 Arrives in Pennsylvania

1694 Penn's wife, Gulielma, dies

1718 Dies on July 30

1681

1718

1681 Receives the charter for Pennsylvania

1684 Returns to England to settle a boundary dispute between Pennsylvania and Maryland

1696 Marries Hannah Callowhill; his son Springett dies

1696	Marries Hannah Callowhill; his son Springett dies.
1699	Returns to Pennsylvania.
1701	Returns to England.
1708	Imprisoned for debts owed to the Ford family.
1712	Arranges to sell Pennsylvania to the crown but suffers a stroke before the deal can be finalized.
1718	Dies on July 30.

Bibliography

BOOKS

Delderfield, Eric R. *Kings and Queens of England*. New York: Stein and Day Publishers, 1972.

Doherty, Kieran. *William Penn: Quaker Colonist*. Brookfield, Conn.: The Millbrook Press, 1998.

Dunn, Mary Maples. *William Penn: Politics and Conscience*. Princeton, NJ: Princeton University Press, 1967.

Fantel, Hans. *William Penn: Apostle of Dissent*. New York: William Morrow and Company, 1974.

Moretta, John A. *William Penn and the Quaker Legacy*. New York: Pearson Longman, 2007.

Pepys, Samuel. *Diary*. London: J.P. Kenyon, 1963.

WEB SITES

Biography.com. "Louis XIV Biography." Available online. URL: http://www.biography.com/articles/Louis-XIV-9386885.

ExplorePAHistory.com. "Overview: The American Revolution: 1765–1783." Available online. URL: http://explorepahistory.com/story.php?storyId=20.

TheMiddleAges.net. "The Black Death: Bubonic Plague." Available online. URL: http://www.themiddleages.net/plague.html.

Nosotro, Rit. "King Louis XIV." Hyperhistory.net. Available online. URL: http://hyperhistory.net/apwh/bios/b2louisXIV.htm.

Penn Treaty Museum. "William Penn and His Pennsylvania Colony." Available online. URL: http://www.penntreatmuseum.org/penn.php.

UCLA.edu. "Brief History during the Snow Era." Available online. URL: http://www.ph.ucla.edu/epi/snow/1859map/newgate_prison_a2.html.

Further Resources

BOOKS

Hinman, Bonnie. *Pennsylvania: William Penn and the City of Brotherly Love*. Hockessin, Del.: Mitchell Lane Publishers, 2007.

Hinman, Bonnie. *Pennsylvania: The Life and Times of William Penn*. Hockessin, Del.: Mitchell Lane Publishers, 2007.

Lutz, Norma Jean. *William Penn: Founder of Democracy*. Philadelphia: Chelsea House Publishers, 2000.

Somerville, Barbara A. *William Penn: Founder of Pennsylvania*. Minneapolis: Compass Point Books, 2006.

DVD

McCally, John. *William Penn and Pennsylvania*. Wynnewood, Penn.: Schlesinger Media, 2006.

WEB SITES

Kids.Net.Au. "William Penn." Available online. URL: http://encyclopedia.kids.net.au/page/wi/William_Penn.

Lazzerini, Rickie. "Pennsylvania History: A Historical Overview." KindredTrails.com. Available online. URL: http://www.kindredtrails.com/Pennsylvania-History-1.html.

NotableBiographies.com. "William Penn Biography." Available online. URL: http://www.notablebiographies.com/Pe-Pu/Penn-William.html.

Samuel, Bill. "William Penn." QuakerInfo.com. Available online. URL: http://www.quakerinfo.com/quakpenn.shtml.

USHistory.org. "Brief History of William Penn." Available online. URL: http://www.ushistory.org/penn/bio.htm.

WilliamPenn.org. "William Penn." Available online. URL: http://www.williampenn.org.

Picture Credits

PAGE

Index

A

American Revolution 89
Amyraut, Moses 30, 31
Anglican Church 25, 34, 42
Anne (Queen of England) 88–
89, 91
arbitrators 53–54
Arran (Earl of) 36
arrests 16–18, 38–39, 50,
88–89

B

Baltimore (Lord) 63, 73–75
Barksdale, Brent 66
birth of William Penn 8
Black Death 10, 33–35, 36
Boccaccio, Giovanni 36
border dispute 63, 73–75, 79
bubonic plague 10, 33–35, 36

C

Callowhill, Hannah. *See* Penn,
Hannah (wife)
Carrickfergus mutiny 36–37
Catholicism 44, 80
Charles I (King of England) 10
Charles II (King of England)
land grant from 56–58
Penn and 32–33, 42

as protector 48
Restoration and 22–24
as tyrant 76–77
Charter of Privileges 85
Charter of West New Jersey 54
charters 54, 56–58, 85
children 65
Church of England 25, 34, 42
civil war (British) 10
clothing 29
colonies, naming of 56, 58–59
Connoy tribe 70
Continental Congress 89
Conventicle Act 44–45
Cromwell, Oliver 10–11, 16–18,
22, 35
Cromwell, Richard 22

D

death of William Penn 92
debt 56–57, 61–62, 87–89
*The Description of West New
Jersey* (Penn) 55
Dickens, Charles 47
diseases 10, 70. *See also* Plague;
Smallpox

E

education 12–14, 24–28, 30,
31–32, 85

103

About the Author

Joanne Mattern is the author of more than three hundred children's books. She has also worked as an editor for several major children's publishers. Mattern lives in New York State with her husband, four children, and an assortment of pets.